Plant Seed, Pull Weed

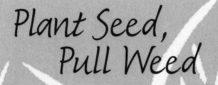

Plant Seed, Pull Weed

Nurturing the Garden of Your Life

GERI LARKIN

HarperOne
An Imprint of HarperCollins*Publishers*

HarperOne

FIRST EDITION

Interior Design: Laura Lind Design

Library of Congress Cataloging-in-Publication Data

Larkin, Geri.
    Plant seed, pull weed : nurturing the garden of your life /
Geri Larkin. — 1st ed.
      p. cm.
    Thematically based on Santideva's Bodhicaryavatara.
    ISBN: 978-0-06-134904-1
    1. Religious life—Buddhism. I. Santideva, 7th cent. Bodhicaryavatara.
II. Title.
BQ4302.L37   2008
294.3'444—dc22   2007047107

08 09 10 11 12 RRD(H) 10 9 8 7 6 5 4 3 2 1

To Jill Collman, Jenny Bridge, and Christie Crowley, three guardian angels of the gardening realm.

> *Blessed are the man and the woman*
> *Who have grown beyond their greed*
> *And have put an end to their hatred*
> *And no longer nourish illusions.*
> *But they delight in the way things are*
> *And keep their hearts open, day and night.*
> *They are like trees planted near flowing rivers,*
> *Which bear fruit when they are ready,*
> *Their leaves will not fall or wither.*
> *Everything they do will succeed.*

—Psalm 1, adapt. Stephen Mitchell,
    A Book of Psalms: Selected and Adopted from the Hebrew

Contents

Thank Yous

In the first two drafts of this book, I thanked "everyone I have ever known" and left it at that. But then I realized that I always read thank-yous and acknowledgments in books because they provide a little inside look into the author's life. Although this book offers plenty of inside looks into my life, it leaves out the people who nurture me day to day. So here are my bows of gratitude to them: First I want to thank Bodhi the dog for not staring me down at 5:00 a.m. to wake me every morning, starting yesterday. I'm so happy for the extra fifteen minutes. Thank you to my children, Sarth Larkin and Jamie Markus, who would be my best friends even if you weren't family. In the last month my life has become increasingly country-and-western-song themed—a roof gone bad, the IRS demanding money, the dog throwing up on my only good shoes. Jamie and Sarth have given me advice and provided constant good cheer, helping me to laugh at the goofiness of my overreacting to any of it (except the shoes: Bodhi, you are now officially on notice).

Sheila Thomson and Nancy Acton have become my own true gossip girls, movie buddies, and let's-catch-the-sun-as-it-sets-over-Lake-Washington go-to friends. How lucky I am to know you in this life!

When you live in the world of quirky singles, having good and constant male friends is a precious gift. Mine are: Koho Vince Anila, Ango Neil Heidrich, David Horowitz, Kassapa, and Bodhidharma

Ron Allen. You are brilliant, funny, generous, and kind beyond measure. Please make as many women friends as possible before you die. We need you.

Even though Andrea Pedolsky left the world of literary agents years ago, she continues to read the small print for me. If we didn't live on opposite coasts, I would beg you to be one of my gossip-movie girls. You are just so, oh, I don't know, cool.

To Eric Brandt, my editor, a final bow of gratitude. In this, our second book together, I have discovered that you get me. I am so helped by your tenacious feedback and your sense of "what the reader needs." Plus, an editor who sends me poems about gardens? It can't get better than that!

My gratitude is immeasurable.

Prologue

Gardening is full of mistakes, almost all of them pleasant and some of them actually instructive.

—Henry Mitchell, *One Man's Garden*

I decided to move from Manhattan to Baltimore for my senior year of college. Johns Hopkins University had professors whose books I admired, and I wanted to get to know the scholars personally. My karma was good that year. In the spring I found an apartment that was basically the second floor of a mansion on an old Southern estate, just southwest of the city. Its owner, Elsie, was ninety-two years old. We took an instant liking to each other. As I moved my boxes of books in, she offered me a job.

"How would you like to be my gardener?"

"I would," I told her. "I would love to be the estate's gardener. The only thing is that I don't know anything about gardening."

She told me it didn't matter. I couldn't hurt anything, really.

Was she wrong!

In my first flurry of hyperactivity I managed to pull up all of her heirloom _____. You can fill in the blank. I pulled up anything that was the slightest bit messy, believing at the time that neatness is all. Only her roses survived. And one or two peony plants I didn't see.

I cut hedges to the ground trying to get their tops even. I killed all the vegetables by waiting until the middle of the afternoon to water them. So first they almost drowned, and then they died of dehydration in the hot sun.

Twice I landed in the emergency room of the local hospital. The first time I was covered with a red rash so itchy I took to chugging Scotch in an effort not to rip the skin off my arms. I don't drink. This means I barely remember making it to the emergency room, where I proceeded to become the day's great mystery disease for the residents.

They had never seen anything like me. The rash was even on my eyelids and inside my ears. After every single resident within a ten-mile radius had examined me, they came up with their diagnosis: I had an exotic rash similar to one a medical student had seen in Africa. Their best guess was that I had somehow managed to pick it up in Mexico the previous summer.

At the end of the afternoon the head ER doctor finally showed up. By then I was sober and completely miserable. My little cubicle was packed with medical students. He took a quick look at me and asked the group what they thought was going on. After they told him, he looked at me again, and then at them.

"She has heat rash."

I went home with Benadryl, enough diaper rash ointment to last the rest of my life, and instructions to stay out of the sun in the middle of the day.

The second time was scarier because I passed out in the heat. That time I got a serious lecture about how the heat and humidity of southern summers are much tougher than the dry heat of the

Australia of my youth. I learned to wear hats, stay in the shade, and drink water constantly.

At the end of the summer Elsie sat me down to tell me, in the sweetest Southern-lady way possible, that I was fired: "Darling, you need not come to work in the morning. I've found someone to take over so you can concentrate on your studies."

Then she gave me two lifetime pieces of advice:

"It would be good not to do any more gardening until you learn about plants."

"Figure out how to live your life in a way that won't kill you prematurely."

I've spent the last thirty years doing both.

Introduction

The most important part of what a garden does lies in the mysterious, subtle, nearly ineffable but heartfelt ways it stirs you to the depths of your soul. That is the magic of gardens. It is only when you are open-hearted in the garden that it can begin to show you what you need to do to take care of it. And what it can do for you. The trick, of course, is how to make that connection.

—Dominique Browning, *Paths of Desire*

Growing up, I was too distracted, being the oldest of five, to learn anything about plants. Well, that isn't exactly true. In first grade, as a summer recess present, my teacher gave me a package of cantaloupe seeds. Since I had no idea what to do with them, I simply threw them all over our yard, doing my best to throw the bulk of the seeds on the strip of dirt next to the garage.

Nothing seemed to happen, so I forgot about them. Then, in mid-July my parents packed my sisters and me into Dad's old Chrysler, and we drove from Cincinnati to my grandmothers' houses in Boston, where we stayed for about a month. It was the middle of the night when we returned to Cincinnati. As we turned into the driveway we were met with loud cracking and splatting sounds, to which my dad added cursing to beat the band. "Jesus Christ!" is the only thing I can repeat. He slammed on the brakes and got out of the car. We piled out after him.

The entire front yard, driveway, side yard, and garage were covered in cantaloupes. Even our sandbox had cantaloupes covering three of four corners. It turned out that Cincinnati dirt, especially dirt in yards directly across the street from cow pastures, is nirvana for cantaloupe seeds.

We spent two days cleaning up the melons and the next three weeks eating them. To this day I pull anything even marginally peach-colored out of salads and off plates before I eat the adjacent food. Even the smell of cantaloupe can make me sit down fast with my head between my knees.

After that summer I was afraid to plant anything. I could only imagine the damage cucumbers or tomatoes could do. Pumpkins would probably take over the house.

Moving through high school and college at the speed of light, I never even thought of getting houseplants. Occasional vases of cut flowers appeared, and I always loved any Valentine's Day roses that found their way to my door. Otherwise I led a green-free life, having no idea what I was missing. I don't think I knew until I was thirty-two whether potatoes grew over or under the ground. (They grow under the ground.)

All that started to shift when meditation found me in 1988. I took a class at the Ann Arbor Temple, and when we did slow-walking meditation in the backyard, I noticed plants for the first time in, maybe, forever. Waves of discoveries hit me hard. All daisies don't look alike. Vegetables ripen at different paces.

Lavender smells delicious in the early morning. You can grow your own kale.

I was so struck by the calming influence meditation had on my upwardly mobile, stress-filled life that I decided to move into the temple. What I wasn't ready for was how busy it was. Temples can be like Grand Central Stations for spiritual crises, and Ann Arborites had plenty of those. From 4:30 a.m. until we dropped dead asleep at 10:00 p.m., we were on call to the universe. In between meetings and counseling were whatever chores we could get done. This meant trying to keep the kitchen and bathrooms clean every day; washing massive loads of laundry; and hanging the loads outside on three clotheslines that ran the length of the backyard. There wasn't time to think about the plants that filled the yard except to lean down and pull an occasional, obvious weed.

And even though there were plants inside the temple, beautiful plants, none of the residents had time to pay them any attention either.

In the middle of our spiritually based chaos, guardian angels would drop in to help: clean up the temple office, make phone calls, complete paperwork, update the mailing list. One of the angels did all these chores and more. She cooked and joked and cleaned and greeted guests. She scolded us when we needed scolding. She told us to take breaks, to go for a walk somewhere away from the building. It would still be standing when we got back. One afternoon, after she had left, we found a sign on one of the temple plants: "The thing about plants is that, without water, they die."

Oops. Plants need to be nurtured and cared for like the rest of us. We had forgotten the lesson of small doings. I decided then and there that I needed to do better by plants. The thing was, I knew nothing about them.

But that was then, and this is now, and except for the canta-loupes, I understand how to love and care for the many plants that keep me company. I know about the importance of regular watering, plant food, and the need to watch out for certain kinds of bugs. I know how to be grateful to plants, having some sense, finally, of how much they give us every day. I know for sure that the world would be a pretty miserable place without them.

Actually, we'd all be dead.

This book is about being as wise and compassionate as we can be, right where we are. Its specific themes come from one of the great classics of Mahayana Buddhism, *The Way of the Bodhisattva,* an eighth-century text by Shantideva. Shantideva was quite the outcast for many years. He didn't start out that way. He started out as a prince. His father, named Victoria's Armor, named his son "armor of peace." In one of the most popular versions of his story, a great teacher appeared to Shantideva in a dream he had as a child, telling him that he would hate the life of a prince. In the other most popular telling, his mother scalded him with water to give him a sample of how much suffering he would experience as a king. Whatever the trigger was, the boy decided early on that he had no interest in running a kingdom. After spending some time as a recluse, he ended up at the Harvard of his time, Nalanda University. There he was a total slacker. In fact, he was known for his expertise in eating, sleeping, and defecating. Apparently nobody liked him, which is saying a lot since the whole purpose of the university was to teach the young men attending it to be good friends to each other and to the world.

In fact, Shantideva was so disliked that, as a practical joke, the rest of the students set him up to give a talk to the whole university community, figuring that he would humiliate himself so badly that he would either have to excuse himself from the place out of shame or he would be kicked out. To make sure his lecture started off as poorly as possible, they didn't provide stairs to access the podium.

Shantideva didn't skip a beat. On the day of his teaching he calmly climbed up onto the podium, looked out at the crowd, and asked the audience of students and teachers what kind of a teaching they wanted. When they replied that they wanted something new, he taught them *The Way of the Bodhisattva*. He focused on the themes of intention, seeing clearly, taming the mind, and being generous, enthusiastic, and patient. With lightness and humor he talked about anger and joy and being vigilant. As he was teaching, Shantideva rose into the air and disappeared so that the only proof that he was in the room was the sound of his voice giving the teachings.

Nobody called him a slacker after that.

Over a millennium later, his teachings continue to be timely. Their underlying theme is *bodhicitta*, or living with a wide-open heart. This heart is fed by calmness, courage, generosity, patience, spunk, and joy. And the more *bodhicitta* is practiced, the more it grows. It feeds our spiritual efforts. It enlarges our hearts.

For this book I mined Shantideva's themes without apology, doing my best to share stories, teachings, and moments when small actions related to his themes have changed a situation for the better. Each one of us is capable of these actions. We can water the plant, feed the kitten, smile at the stranger, amuse the crying baby. We can share food, volunteer at a food bank, laugh with a friend until we hiccup. As we do these things, moment by moment, the world heals. So do we.

This work can be hard. What am I saying? It *is* hard! It is hard to be calm, especially these days. It is hard to have courage. I have days when I'm so wired I can't even spell the word *patience*. It takes a lot of energy to be joyful in the middle of a society riddled with whining. In the same way, gardening is hard work. Weeding, whether it means letting go of the destructive thoughts parading through our brains or pulling up the bindweed that has taken over our entire lawn in the last twenty-four hours, is a never-ending, backbreaking job. Watering plants takes more skill than anyone who doesn't water plants can guess. Knowing what plants to grow where takes patience and planning, vigilance and energy—all of Shantideva's themes.

As we learn, though, to give ourselves up to the hard work and to take on Shantideva's teachings as our own personal guide to living a clearheaded life, a funny thing happens. We actually see the powerful impact that comes from taking his advice. We notice more, appreciate more, and fall in love with all of it.

We become the master gardeners of our lives.

We learn how to be so focused doing something that miracles can spring up through our brain cells. We may go out into our yard to weed, only to stand up three hours later with a half-written business plan in our head, the one for the business that will, finally, pay off our college loans. We may suddenly realize that we are supposed to run for office or tell someone we love them or go get a dog from the pound. We might figure out what is missing from the last painting we finished. We might grab a phone to call in an apology that is ten years overdue.

The secret to this transformation is to engage in our gardening small step by small step, or small doing by small doing. This is how we stay out of emergency rooms because of a heat rash or heat-stroke. My friend Nat Needle is a brilliant songwriter who first taught me about small doings. When we were in a seminary together, his focus was Buddhist songs. I loved them because they could be both wise and hilarious, and they helped me enormously as I tried to remember Buddha's teachings. His "Truckin' down the Eightfold Path" got me through my first oral exam, the one where I was supposed to have memorized everything from key Buddhist concepts and the full annual schedules of the Ann Arbor and Chicago Zen Buddhist temples to milestones in my teacher's life.

Nat was the first person I ever met who, through small acts, changed us all for the better. A kind note here, a small gift there. A paperweight he gave me, the one that says, "Relax, my darling," still sits on my desk fifteen years later. One summer Nat decided to compose a CD's worth of songs, as I remember it, to help raise funds for the Ann Arbor Zen Buddhist Temple, where we were studying. His output was big-themed songs that ranged from jazz to reggae to ballads. A tango about the king of heartbreak, a calypso about the need to "pull the arrow right out" instead of asking so many questions about it that we die in the process. When the temple's resident dharma teacher, Haju Murray, heard them, she asked if he would also write a simple song about ordinary things. The result was a song called "Small Doin's." Its message is this: when we completely focus on what is right in front of us—brushing our messy hair (if there), drying the wet dish, putting the seat down again—we are expressing a deep wisdom and compassion, called *prajnaparamita,* which becomes a way for us to help the Earth to be a better place. Think about a time when you saw a tea ceremony or an artist at work or somebody completely focused on getting the recipe right, and you will have a taste of what I mean. There is so much beauty and quiet energy in the movement that it feels sacred. It is sacred. Through small doings we waste less, argue less (since we listen better), sing more, and are happier. We know what needs weeding and what needs to be left alone.

Small doings, it turns out, can be hard work. It is much easier to leave the seat up, our hair messy, the phone call unreturned. But laziness doesn't help the world—or our own lives. Small doings, by contrast, can and do. When we simply focus on doing what is right in front of us, act by act, our hearts open. I don't know why this is true, I only know that it is, and that over time a shift takes place. Our brains morph from being crammed full of our personal version of anger, greed, and delusion to being filled with a clearheadedness that naturally leads us to doing exactly what needs doing in every situation we find ourselves in.

For those of us who are impatient, this process can feel painfully gradual. It took me five years of hard, constant spiritual work to have a first glimpse of completely clear thinking. When it happened it felt like a lens had fallen away from my eyes, making a clear spot, if you will, in the gunk. Over time the clear spot has grown as I've trusted myself more. And even though I have miles to go before I sleep, this awakeness has made some truths clear. One is that we are all inherently awake. Another is that we really are spirit made flesh. We are holy. Clearheadedness has taught me not to predict the impact of any act of kindness because you just never know.

As you and I rush deeper into our era of plugged ears, speed, and multitasking, finding a path to the quiet of awakeness becomes a mandate if we are to stay sane, not to mention pleasant. Embracing a life filled with small doings is one such path. As we learn to focus, at least sometimes, on what is right in front of us, we find we can let go of the generalized anxiety that invades us. We remember what it is like to feel calm, to play, and to laugh at silly small things without having a need to go anywhere or be with anyone else to complete our lives. We become bodhisattvas, Buddhist saints, if you will, responding naturally to the need for help that is everywhere, whether it surfaces in the form of a puppy asking for breakfast, a shrub that needs water, or a bathroom floor that needs washing. Chaos becomes beauty, lethargy energy, insolvable problems solvable. We learn to love, one kiss at a time. Small doings writ large can save this sweet planet we call home.

Where to start on this path from muddy to clear? Right where we are. For me, these days are plant filled. I started working in a nursery two years ago partly because, as you now know, I have a history of terrible luck with plants. They either die immediately or plot to take over two surrounding states as soon as I turn my back. Determined to break this curse before I die, I plunked myself down in the middle of plant lovers, growers, and groupies. I survived by paying attention to what is right in front of me. As a result I've been wildly happy and have found ways to genuinely be of help to the world I'm in. It is a good life, a lucky one, one that every day yields surprises, gifts, and lessons to learn.

In the end *Plant Seed, Pull Weed* is a hymn to an awakened life—a life that is its own full and beautiful garden. The themes are ones that can lead us into the land of quiet happiness even as we are surrounded by increasing chaos. They are the themes that have taken me from a know-nothing, estate-destroying workhorse to a person who can make her living as a gardener. As my gardening skills have improved, I've fallen deeper in love with the Earth and everything on it. I've become, in Mary Oliver's words, "a bride married to amazement." It doesn't get better, this blooming of a life.

Regarding the format of this book, since Shantideva starts with clear intention, that is the topic of chapter 1. Without intention, nothing happens. We don't change. We stay our miserable, whining selves. (Okay, maybe that is just me.) A garden never gets grown. In life, in gardening, we need to have a sense of the direction we want to go. It makes for a deeper, less frenetic life, one in which we aren't constantly pulled in different directions. Intention is a huge antidote to the exhaustion of too many directions at once.

From there, Shantideva takes on hesitation. We need to stop hesitating. We'll make mistakes in our lives and in our gardening. Okay. That is how we learn. Chapter 2 is about hesitation. There is no day like today, no time like right now, to start doing what needs doing. Hug that person who needs it. Drink that cup of tea without a book in your hand. Say something to the lonely woman at the bus stop. Pull the three thistles in the front of your building before they explode. Excitement can't happen, joy can't happen, gardens can't grow, if we hesitate.

Chapter 3 is about the hard work of seeing what is right in front of us. This becomes the true first step in the growing of a genuine garden as opposed to simply filling spaces with whatever happens to be within reach. If we don't learn how to see clearly, we'll never clean up the destructive thinking and behavioral patterns that prevent us from living a joy-filled life.

of God

Generosity, a grand theme in all of Zen, is the topic of chapter 4. It feeds relationships, self-esteem, world peace. Gardening feeds generosity. If we have any success at all, we'll end up with too many vegetables and garden plots that need to be periodically cleaned out. True gardeners hate to compost anything someone else might be able to use. If you are like me, you'll find yourself first giving away plants, then pots, then clothes and furniture you don't really need. Generosity builds on itself because it just plain feels good.

Every garden needs our enthusiastic effort to survive and thrive. So does every life. Chapter 5 is about enthusiasm. Shantideva emphasizes it as a sort of spiritual grease that makes everything else in life not just doable but fun. In my experience the people who put all of themselves into whatever they are doing are happier than people who spend their lives multitasking. Plus, their gardens thrive because they've noticed the bugs that need to be removed, the weeds that need pulling, the plants that need more sun and less watering. In this chapter enthusiasm appears in the form of a young artist, jaimie healy. By the time you read this book, you might be hearing about her through the media. She is that talented.

Chapter 6 reminds us how weed filled our lives are, from lines of thinking that will never do us any good to the literal weeds that will ultimately choke the landscape if you and I don't get out there, tools in hand.

Shantideva spends a lot of time teaching about patience in *The Way of the Bodhisattva*. Chapter 7 is about patience. As an impatient person, I will need this teaching to my last breath. In my fifties, I'm grateful that I'm not as impatient as I was in my thirties when my nickname was "Hurricane." I've learned that in spite of everything I can think or do, every season has its own rhythm. I can't force my little garden to grow any faster than it will, any more than I can wake up one morning and say to myself, "Today is full-enlightenment day. Better get out the good dress." Gardens don't work that way. Neither does spiritual growth.

Driving impatience? For many of us, it is anger, the most insidious mind-weed of all. Chapter 8 covers anger of a particular form, one that seems to be showing up more and more. I call it the mean-girl syndrome. Sadly, I see it everywhere.

The harvest of harvests, joy, is the theme of chapter 9. Shantideva teaches us that feeding joy is critical. Gardens and gardening feed joy. So do puppies and raindrops on roses and bright copper kettles. This chapter is about how surprisingly easy it can be to feed joy once we give ourselves the gift of believing we deserve it. We do. The chapter also shares some of the intimacy of joy, an emotion that can surface right here, right now, no matter what else is going on.

Finally, Shantideva teaches vigilance, the topic of *Plant Seed, Pull Weed*'s last chapter. We need to pay constant attention to how we are living our lives. Again, hard work. I've always found that stories of other people's vigilance help me to stay on track. Most of the last chapter of this book is about Wangari Maathai, who single-handedly and against all odds led a green revolution in Kenya. Just thinking about her always gives me the energy to move into the next small doing that needs my attention. Yesterday that meant pulling those thistles in front of the building. Today it means e-mailing a friend to tell her not to be afraid to go into a seminary program. There is no downside, I will tell her. Later this afternoon it will mean writing a check for twenty-five dollars to a nonprofit trying to end child prostitution. It is a small check. I'm not Eudora Welty, after all. But I'll send them something with every paycheck I get. That way they will know that some woman outside of Seattle, one with a constant grin and a grateful twinkle in her eye, is cheering them on with everything she's got. Every day.

Casing the Landscape: Developing a Clear Intention

Most gardeners just start digging holes and stuffing things in (such as the fastest growing maples and poplars they can find) and are perfectly happy for about three years. Then it dawns on them that the garden does not excite them much, and this revelation usually occurs about the first time they see pictures of a fine garden constructed on other principles.
—Henry Mitchell, *Small Gardens: The Big Picture*

We can be happy. Right here. Right now. In fact, this seems to be the great cosmic prank. We look for happiness everywhere instead of right in front of us. The teacup I am holding in my hand, at first glance, is a small, plain, white, round, ceramic cup. But as I take time to really look, it has every color. Blues in the shadows. Some purple. Pink along the edges. Sparkling spots where the light directly hits it. And the tea, a green tea, ranges from a light gold to a deep caramel with shadows that constantly shift as though they were on a tiny dancing lake. It smells of the earth, tastes like the earth, and warms me to my toes on a cold fall morning. All this in a simple cup of tea. How can I not be happy?

Having my foot in a cast doesn't take away from the taste of the tea. In the same way, facing a pileup of bills won't erase the sun shining through the front window or the musky smell of someone's fire in a fireplace. It has taken me a while to realize that the problems of our lives don't erase the nonproblem parts of our lives—the flowers, the trees, the stripes of light on a wall. These things always surround us, even in prison cells and basement apartments.

There is, however, a catch. (You knew this was coming.) To be happy, we first need to intend to be happy.

Maybe fifteen years ago, back in my hand-tailored-suit management-consultant days, my boss sent me to a daylong business conference at the local community college. Its theme was team building. At first I thought I was being punished since nobody else from the firm was asked to participate. By the end of the day I understood that he had given me a gift. It took a while for the magnitude of the gift to sink in. I'm like that.

The day does not start well. We are separated into groups of eight and told to sit at circular tables that have crayons on them. Groan. Double groan. Give me a handwritten excuse to get out of here now. Help me disappear. Anything but the crayons. I am at a table of men, mostly bankers and academics. When they see the crayons they look as frantic as I feel.

It gets worse.

At the center of each table is a huge pile of blank paper. Beside the piles are Magic Markers in every color. We are back in kindergarten.

We sit down, gingerly. Nobody speaks. We don't even look at each other.

The first speaker of the day is a young energetic man from the Ford Motor Company. One of their up-and-comers. He starts raving about some management consultant, Peter Senge, from Boston. I'm already thinking, "Not another management consultant with a quick fix. Kill me now." But because I'm too chicken to get up in front of everyone else, and I don't want to let my crayon-sharing team down, I stay through the rest of the rave. Senge, he tells us, has woven together a formula for helping companies to function better.

I don't know about the other tables. At mine, we are still looking down. Eye contact might set off laughter. We have heard this promise too many times.

The place to start is with intentions, he tells us. Our own. By this time the young fellow is running around the room because he can't keep his excitement in one place. "Where is my camera?" I think. I want this on film for the days when I can't get started. Just watching him is making us all smile. He is contagious.

We are instructed to take a piece of blank paper and to either list or sketch where we intend to be in ten years. We are to include our homes, the climate, the geography, our livelihood. The people we will be surrounded by. To keep us going, the day's organizers have put M&M's, cauldrons of coffee, and cases of Diet Coke within reach.

We have forty-five minutes. Since I've always loved crayons, I make sketches and write vivid descriptions of everything that will be in my life ten years out. My tablemates write their intentions as outlines. Each theme has subcategories, and each subcategory has measurable accomplishments. They must have gone to the same business school. Their outlines look identical when I try to read them, uninvited, upside down. The room is quiet while we concentrate. After a while the facilitator starts talking again. The only thing we have to do to get from where we are to what we have described, he tells us, is to set clear intentions. In other words, we have to decide we really want what we have already written down. Then every time we have to make a choice related to these intentions, we simply make the one that gets us closer to it. Feed the images we've drawn in our minds. It is that simple. Companies are the same, he says, and proceeds to share Senge case studies of how clear intentions, acted out, have changed companies for the better.

Listening, I am not convinced, although the exercise was fun and the case studies are interesting. Too many other variables could have affected the companies' shifts. I shove the sketches into a book I have with me and promptly forget about them until ten years later when, in a flurry of energy, I decide to give away all of my books. Okay, not all of them. All but one bookshelf worth, which quickly becomes one bookcase worth, but at least I can walk through the living room again.

I found the sketches.

I was literally living the life I had described. I had started a meditation center. I lived in a wooded area near mountains and the ocean. I was happy. My kids were grown and happy. Even Bodhi the puppy had appeared. He looks like the puppy in my picture, the one that looks more like a stuffed teddy bear than anything else.

In Buddhism, intention matters. In fact, this is where Shantideva starts. "Intend," he tells us. Postponing making intentions is a big mistake. With everything we may hope to do in our lifetimes, it is important to remember that we won't live forever. So we need to focus on our intentions now, not later. What do we really want? Do we want to mature spiritually? Do we want to grow a garden filled with smells and colors? What? Zen master Seung Sahn used to admonish his students: "No one knows when he will die. It could be next year or next week or the next five minutes."

We need to decide.

And then we need to go easy on ourselves. This can be a difficult task in a society that isn't easy on anyone. It helps to accept that we will make mistakes headed in the direction of our intentions because that's what happens to people. The measure of our sincerity, whether we are spiritual seekers, gardeners, or both, rests on our intention. As long as our hearts are sincere and our intentions are kind, we are okay. Progress, if you will, is being made. Since I am a mistake-making machine, some days my intention to wake up for the sake of the world is literally the only thing that keeps me on my path.

Humans have the impulse to live a life that reflects who we genuinely are, starting with our values and moving out to our interests. This
is the life that makes us happiest. We already have the impulse to be
helpful to each other. Our job is to simply feed these impulses,
regardless of what is happening around us.

The first time I physically panicked about the state of the world
and not knowing what I could do to help was when I was staying in
a Zen temple in Chicago, twelve years ago. To tell you the truth, I
can't remember what triggered the panic, but when it hit I was
floored. My whole body shook, I was sick to my stomach, tears flew
out of my eyes. Between the heaves, my whole body sobbed.
The state of the world and how we had come to not take care of each
other was a reality that I couldn't comprehend without being physically sick. It was terrifying. The earth was dying. We were dying. We
were putting our sons in prison and letting our grandparents starve.
We were killing each other. We were killing ourselves. And this was
all before September 11.

I went to my teacher for help. His response was simple. Our job, he
told me, is to keep doing our work. If we are the last people on Earth, we
can still be kind and we can still be happy. We can still be helpful. For
example, even if all the trees on the earth are dying and we know that it
is our last day on the planet, our job is to keep planting trees.

"Go plant a tree," he told me.

Whatever else is going on, we need to have the intention to help
each other the best we can, through thick and thin, through our

aging and dying, through the Earth's own ebbs and flows. And we can do this, not by big actions—unless we have access to big resources—but through simple acts of kindness. By simply saying yes to a situation that can use our help.

A colleague falls on hard times. We bring her food. A friend is moving. We take her castoffs to a local nonprofit.

In the Maitreya seminary where I was trained, we were taught to simply say yes to requests, without a need to find out the details of the request. In this way we would become more available to be of service to the world moment by moment. We were taught that the same yes would lead us along a path of happiness. It would feed our noble intentions.

This has led to some wild rides, I admit. Most recently, I was stocking Dusty Miller plants at the nursery where I work when one of the managers approached me to ask if I would be willing to be the sidekick to a local wunderkind, Ciscoe Morris, while he did a live radio show about plant care. In the Northwest gardening subculture, Ciscoe Morris has the status of a rock star. He used to be the manager of grounds and landscaping for Seattle University. Ciscoe is a certified arborist, a master gardener, and a teacher at many of Seattle's local colleges. He knows more about organic gardening than anyone I have ever met, and he is forever advising people, when they have a decision to make, to choose the environmentally friendly route. He is a slight, weathered ball of energy who has a way of solving gardening problems with an entertaining combination of

compassion and chutzpah. His television shows, radio shows, and
weekly public appearances can become mob scenes. Part of it is his
knowledge. People can rarely stump him with their questions. The
man is an encyclopedia of all things plant, shrub, and tree. Part of it
is his obvious heart. He loves plants and he loves people. Part of it is
his sense of humor.

Yes. I said I would do the show. Only later did I learn that it was
three hours long and that it was supposed to be a conversation
between experts.

I freaked.

But I did it.

And even though, going in that morning, I prayed that most of
the questions would be about petunias, geraniums, and ivy, my three
areas of knowledge, when there wasn't a single question about any of
them, I discovered I knew way more than I thought. We always do.
And I had the time of my life, laughing with Ciscoe and acting as his
bodyguard when he left. I was honored to see what he was really like
one-on-one. What struck me most was how closely he paid attention
to the questions asked. He made really sure he got as much information as possible about a gardener's situation before he responded. As
a result he always had an answer, in spite of people going to great
lengths to stump him. Halfway through the radio show, a woman
walked up to our table, set seven leaves down, and said, "Help!" It
was obvious that something was wrong with each leaf. Some were
curled. Some were half-brown. Some had splotches. Even though we

were on the radio, Ciscoe took time to really look at each leaf before he reacted. A half minute of silence on the radio couldn't compete with clearly seeing what was going on.

He proceeded to tell her exactly what was wrong with each leaf. Overwatering was killing her laurel. Bugs were eating a heuchera. The only person who even came close to stumping him that morning was a little girl who wanted to know how long Venus flytraps live. Her question wasn't an easy one. Venus flytraps are pretty complicated. They need a lot of moisture and depend on insects for their nutrients. In the wild they live only in bogs in the Carolinas.

Flytraps look like big toothy smiles. When the smiles open you can see short stiff hairs that are so sensitive to touch that if anything bends them, even a little, the smiley mouth snaps shut, trapping whatever it is. The mouth doesn't close all the way at first. There is a slight pause and then, slam!

Flytraps are also picky. If it swallows a nut, a small stick, or a piece of a McDonald's kids' meal toy, it will spit it back out by the end of the day. All this means that, to survive, flytraps need insects that are just right. Not too big, not too small. If they are too small they can fly back out of a plant's mouth. Too big and they force the mouth to stay a little open, which means that bacteria and mold can get into the flytrap. This is not a pretty sight. Basically, the plant turns black, rots, and falls to the ground. If you own one and want to hand-feed it, you need to make sure that the mouth really closes, and tightly, over its meal. Then you have to squeeze it in different places to make the insect move as if it were alive. That's what speeds up the digestive process. A lot of work for one tiny, toothy, smiley face.

With one "just right" insect, a flytrap can live for almost two weeks. They live best in old aquariums or fishbowls that are small enough to keep humid at all times. They need sun for at least two hours a day. Warm and moist, a plant can live for a long time. Even underwater if it has to.

But no hamburger. No tofu. And for sure no fish can pass through its lips.

Ciscoe had no idea what the little girl knew about flytraps. He didn't know if she had one, was buying one, or was thinking about buying one. So he gave her a perfect Zen answer: "It depends." He told her some of the requirements, emphasizing that the main thing was to feed the plant food that was "just right." If she intended to have a healthy flytrap, she needed to learn about the plants first. Her mother would help. That way she could have two toothy grins that would last—hers and her plant's. And then, to thank her for having the courage to stand up and ask him a question, he gave her a huge flower in a pot. With that, yet another Ciscoe admirer was hatched.

As we set our intentions and say yes to the things that come our way, these small actions shift our lives. It is pretty amazing when you think about it—how our lives are transformed act by act. Last week a young Seattle teen came back from spending two years living with Buddhist monks in Cambodia. His mother took him there because he had gotten involved with drugs and gangs and she was terrified for his life. When he was asked about the biggest change in him, he said that he shifted from focusing on what he wanted to being grateful for what he already had. The shift happened when he finally, after months of fighting it, simply said yes to living in a temple.

The world of gardening depends on this combination of intention and saying yes. Great gardens start out with clear intentions. What do you want, really?

A place for a quiet cup of tea? A spot for your dog to pee? Somewhere your partner can woodwork or grill or knit? A corner where a teen can sulk without having to defend the sulking or without even being seen, for that matter?

What do we want? The details matter. Small details matter. Coming up with them can be great fun. Intention on paper becomes a plan, whether it is crayon sketches on blank paper, a wish list, or detailed drawings on graph paper.

Whether it is our garden, our livelihood, our relationships, or our spirituality, it helps to share our intentions, to say them out loud. Senge has convinced me, as has my own life, that being clear here helps our futures to unfold in a positive way. Plus, we never know when our intentions, spoken out loud, will motivate someone else to expand their life in some way. A while back I worked part-time in a sweet little bookstore in Kirkland, Washington. Stonehouse. Every person who walked through the door was warmly welcomed by the owners. It was their ministry. The elderly toothless man who had a tendency to burst into song was just as welcome as the Peruvian shaman who just moved to Seattle, who was just as welcome as the young mothers who would come to shop for holiday or birthday gifts for their families.

One day a young girl came in and headed to the store's small witchcraft section. She was there for a long time. Finally I walked back and asked if I could help her with something. She told me that her high school had become very dangerous. She wanted to climb the hill behind the school and put a safety spell on the whole place. She didn't want anyone to be scared anymore—not the students, not the teachers. She didn't want to see the police in the halls and at the front doors in the mornings.

I helped her to find a spell, and she helped me with intention. I vowed to do everything I could to help the world's teenagers to feel more safe in a not-so-safe world. I support my friends who work directly with them. Jaimie and Lisa, who mentor girls not much younger than they are. Pauline, who, following her retirement, volunteers in the city of Detroit's schools.

Sarah, who gave up formal ministry to teach in an inner-city school. Sarth, as he drives two hours each way at least once a month to spend time with young men in a federal prison. They need us. They deserve better, these children of ours. All I needed was the reminder of a fourteen-year-old looking for a protective spell.

Rolling Up Your Sleeves: Transcending Hesitation

Since the beginning of this love I have felt that unless I gave myself up to it entirely, without any restrictions, with all my heart, there was no chance for me whatever.... But what is it to me whether my chance is slight or great? I mean, must I consider this when I love? No—no reckoning; one loves because one loves. Then we keep our heads clear ... nor do we hide our feelings, nor smother the fire and light, but simply say: Thank God, I love.

—Vincent van Gogh, *Dear Theo: The Autobiography of Vincent van Gogh*

For many of us who hate to fly, and that number appears to be increasing by the hour, only a lover can entice us to fly from Seattle to Boston and back. For others of us, it may take the illness of a son or daughter or the birth of a grandchild. Koans get me onto a plane.

Koans are crazy questions that are most helpful when asked by a spiritual teacher in a formal interview. Here are two well-known examples: "What is the sound of one hand clapping?" "What was your face before your mother was born?"

I have loved koans for years. I think it is because I've learned, through constant failure, that the correct responses to these questions can never come from my thinking mind. Conceptual thinking only gets me into trouble. Correct responses have to come from a deeper wisdom, a heart-based wisdom. When a correct response pops up, it feels like a birthday party going on in my head—a three-dimensional happy surprise.

And even though, on paper, there are lots of teachers who profess to have koan competence, I've only discovered a handful of teachers who genuinely get this stuff. Three of them are in Boston.

So I get on airplanes to see them. And I stay at places like the Cambridge Zen Center, where I can formally sit in meditation and have interviews with teachers who have the skill to show me where I still need to work on myself with a serious spiritual scrub brush. In the fall of 2006 I headed to Boston for five days of abbey life. And interviews. The first was with a meticulous and clearheaded dharma teacher. It was an instant reminder of the need to transcend hesitation whenever he asked me a question. On the one hand, the second I started to think about a response to the questions he was asking me, I knew I was wrong and the interview was over. On the other hand, when I leaned in and just went for it, we had a veritable koan party, one that lasted for my entire stay. Shifting from brain to heart is worth bumpy flights squeezed between two unhappy people who have been traveling too long.

In Buddhism we are taught to "just do it" in any situation.
Buddha taught this through a very funny story in which he asked
a student this question: If he was pierced with an arrow, would he
start asking who shot it and where did it come from, or would he
just pull the bloody thing out of his chest?

You know the answer.

So we practice leaning in to whatever situation we find ourselves
in, without the need to overanalyze or criticize. And as we learn to lean
in to one situation, it becomes easier and easier to lean in to other
situations—into all situations, in fact. Back to Boston. Koan practice
prepared me to take on a lifelong monster, the Boston public transportation system's subways. Before I arrived in the city, I had decided
to either walk or take a bus to the Institute of Fine Arts, where I
wanted to spend afternoons. I told myself I would simply ignore the
existence of the subways.

That my fear of the transit system was irrational didn't make it
go away. It must come from getting lost in the system when I was a
small child visiting my grandparents in the city. Or maybe not. I just
know I've had nightmares about the underground all my life, ones
where snakes cover the walkways, spiders cover the walls, all the
stairways lead nowhere, and there are only skeletons in the subway
cars. The dreams usually show up on nights before exams or public-
speaking engagements. Perhaps you know these nightmares. The
best I can figure is that my mother or grandmother must have
decided to abandon me when I was, say, four years old, and it was

so traumatic that I remember nothing but the fear. That my mother and grandmothers are kind, generous, and saintly means nothing. Nightmares are nightmares.

In Boston, I mastered the subway. It took an hour and several wrong directions, but in the end the subway was mine. And I loved it. Even better, on my first ride, halfway to the art museum I looked down to see that someone had carefully set a pass smack in the middle of the seat next to me. It was good for three days. So I ended up riding all over the city, spending extra time in stations where someone was shouting poetry, singing loudly, or playing a musical instrument. I discovered that even when the subway was the most crowded, other riders always gave me the room I needed to get in and out of every car.

Why do we hesitate? Maybe we'll feel stupid or embarrassed when situations don't play out the way we want them to. Maybe we'll be losers. But the Buddha taught that there are no losers. Not a single one of us, even on our worst saggy, fat, love-handled, pizza-bellied, bad-breath days is a loser. We are, each of us, Buddha. All the time. As such, we need to transcend hesitation. When we do, all sorts of wonderful surprises head our way.

Years ago a friend of mine asked me to sit on a panel on diversity for incoming students of the MBA program in one of this country's top three business schools. Because he was my friend, I said yes and promptly forgot all about the promise.

A week before the event he called me to remind me.

"What should I talk about?" I asked.

Anything that'll help a business student be more skillful in the world of business, he told me. I decided to talk about a surprise teaching I got from my Zen teacher at my ordination. When we were ordained in the Maitreya Buddhist Seminary in Toronto, the final rite of passage was to receive personal advice from the Zen masters witnessing the ordination. Most of the advice given to me was predictable: aphorisms like "Be grateful" or "Remember how lucky you are" or straightforward advice like "Please take your role as a teacher seriously." All sweet, forgettable words. When I got to Sunim, the last person in the lineup, he said to me, "Learn to lose."

In an instant I knew he had given me the best advice of my lifetime. I needed to let go of my opinions and preconceived notions so I could be completely free to respond to whatever was happening *in any situation*. By learning to lose, I would see more clearly, to everyone's benefit, because I wouldn't be tangled up in the person I call "me." For example, I would know whether to stay and argue or to recognize that a conversation was over and it was time to walk away. Sunim promised me that by learning to lose, I would be able to do these things without getting too caught up in wanting to control outcomes. I would pay better attention to my own behavior. Was I listening? Was I being kind? Generous? Clear? By learning to lose, I would be better able to see what was really going on for the other person or people. Was she really angry or just scared? Was he done talking or just too frustrated to stay in the conversation? I wouldn't take difficult situations personally. This was a huge gift since I have historically been very good at taking just about anything personally, including the weather. When I learned to lose, what I needed to do would always be clear, wise, and skillful. It would be the right thing to do.

Since skepticism is embedded in my cell structure, I immediately started testing out his advice, and I'll be damned if that man wasn't right. I started asking people to correct my understanding of situations. Was I missing something? What advice did they have for me? Their responses have *always* provided additional information that shifted the situation. When I later worked part-time to help pay some of the temple's bills, a young woman late for work on a regular basis who had been labeled insolent was actually trying to take care of her sister's three small children while her sister went through rehab. Her insolence was exhaustion. A fellow management consultant who threw a megatantrum when I disagreed with him on a project was wrestling with a marriage gone bad and I reminded him of his wife. Not okay, but at least I knew where he was coming from. Learning to lose, I became more skillful and was able to negotiate better contracts with and for clients. I found structural problems in strategic plans and marketing strategies much faster. As a side benefit, this letting go gave me a new kind of freedom. I realized that I didn't need to foresee problems as much, and I discovered unlimited resources and help in solving difficulties that popped up in my own life and in whatever work situation I was in.

I decided to tell the MBA students about Sunim's advice. But when I got to the school, I felt completely overwhelmed. Not only was the very large auditorium crammed with students, professors, and the dean, the four other people on the panel were renowned leaders in the world of business, including the first Latino to head a major international corporation and an African American man who had single-handedly turned around a big chunk of the U.S. auto industry.

I was a no-name.

The others offered wonderful advice, the kind you want to keep in your top desk drawer in case you ever need an instant pep talk. I didn't even have notes with me.

When I was handed the microphone, I couldn't talk I was so nervous. Then two words, *transcend hesitation*, popped into my head, and I let loose. I told everyone I was so nervous it was quite possible that I might pee on myself and if I did I'd appreciate their ignoring it. The dead silence that followed told me that I had inadvertently gotten their attention. The room was so quiet I actually heard a pin drop. Then I told Sunim's story, knowing that it ran against the grain of much else that they would be taught. I asked each student to try to drop their assumptions about the situations they would find themselves in and just focus, to put their energy into being fully present, and trust that in that presence there would be correct guidance. I promised that they would someday thank me.

When I finished there was only quiet. Then, polite applause. So much for transcending hesitation.

room just this side of mortified, I found a

me in the hall. At the end of the line, the

 .n them the gift of the day," he told me. "More

 .., you have given me a huge gift. I'm going to start telling

your story in my talks because people need to hear it."

We just never know.

Transcending hesitation is about living a life without regret because we've always stepped into the ring. It can save situations, relationships, lives. Wesley Autrey is a New York City man, a construction worker, who a few days ago leaped in front of a subway train to save the life of a complete stranger. The man had suffered a seizure, which had caused him to fall onto the tracks. Autrey lay over his body to protect him as the train went over both of them. Autrey's two young daughters watched the whole thing from the platform.

Both men survived.

Even better, when we transcend hesitation we make life easier for everyone around us because they don't have to get lost in the land of guessing what we want or don't want. This is true whether they are partners, co-workers, children, or bosses. Landscaping in the Northwest's constant winter rain creates an ecstatic appreciation for instant decisions on the part of my boss. Cindi, our crew leader, never hesitates. Her fast reactions save time and make for significantly shorter workdays. When we walk around a yard at the beginning of a day to scope things out, she just points and says, "Pull it." Or, "Chop it down," for the plants and bushes where I wonder what is most needed. So we do. The yards always look better, if sometimes a little naked, when we are finished. Cindi chooses death with dignity for plants that are going downhill. She doesn't want us to waste our time, or our clients' money, trying to keep a dying plant in the land of the living. She is also great with mistakes. When I make one, I tell her, she fixes it, and we move on. No scolding. No "I told you so." We just do the next thing. I love her directness because I don't have to guess. She helps me keep my karma clean because I never feel an impulse to pretend that I know something I don't know. She lets me make mistakes, knowing I'm doing the best I can. That I'll screw up, that we all will, is a given. Okay. We fix our mistakes as best we can, apologize when it is needed, and move on. Doing this, we allow everyone else involved in whatever is happening to move on as well.

Working at the nursery, I discovered that customers also appreciate it when I don't hesitate to show them plants that will work in their containers or gardens. I just treat their needs as koans and zoom in on what would be most helpful. Sometimes this means heading for a master gardener because the customer needs more detailed information to make a planting decision. Sometimes this means simply going with my gut and heading for particular tables to pick up pots of plants they can put into their carts. My system always works.

Especially in moments when I know I would have hesitated if I hadn't simply leaned in to the situation.

One morning I saw a woman standing next to the biggest table of petunias. She was just staring at them. I first noticed her as I pushed a huge rack of geraniums to the front of the store. When I headed back almost an hour later with an empty rack, she was still there. So I walked up to her and without thinking said, "You know, I normally don't hug customers since I'm not the hugging type … but do you need one?"

She nodded yes. I could see she was crying. So I leaned in some more. "How can I help?"

She started crying hard. The petunias and I just stood still, witnesses to her heartbreak. When she was able to catch her breath, she told me that her cat had died a week ago and that she couldn't stop crying. Her co-workers were tired of it. Her friends were also getting impatient with her. But he was family.

"Let's make him a memorial garden."

We spent the rest of the morning working side by side, putting one together. We chose catnip (of course) and orange pansies the color of his fur. We picked out a couple of hebes and some Mexican grass that would sway in the wind in a way that would make it impossible for any cat to ignore. We found a ceramic Cheshire cat to tuck into the corner of the garden. By the end of our adventure she was half-smiling and I was realizing how healing a visit to a nursery can be.

Within the month I found myself helping three other families design memorial gardens—for a parrot, a dog, and a baby deer two kids had found at the back of their property. Each time I silently thanked that woman at the petunias for showing me what would work.

Leaning in. So many love stories grow out of a person having the courage to move past hesitation to make that first move. That there aren't more love stories tells me that we are, all of us, giving in to hesitation. For five years I was in love with a man who, I am pretty sure, was also in love with me. We enjoyed doing the same quirky things. We have the same political bent. We both meditate. We even went to the same college. Of the thousands of letters I've received in my life, the handful I received from him have always made the "I'll just hold on to this" cut. For a few of those years we had legitimate reasons for keeping our mouths shut. He was married for the first two that I knew him; I made a commitment to move away for one of them. Today, when friends ask me who the love of my life is, I don't know the answer. Had I spoken my heart to Joseph, it might have been him. And even though I haven't seen him in years, a part of me wonders what would have happened if either of us had moved through hesitation. When a friend told me that he remarried last year I was happy for his new partner. She has herself a mighty catch.

When I moved to the city of Detroit in 2002, I had learned about hesitation and how to transcend it. Throwing myself into the urban living experience, I took art workshops at the Detroit

Institute of Art, rode my Schwinn bicycle whenever I could, became an almost regular at the Eastern Market. I went to Friday night movies at the institute and wrote at a tiny café with my dharma brother Bija Drew Wright. I don't know exactly when it happened, but I do remember waking up one morning and looking out into the frozen street and feeling overwhelmed with love for the city—that feeling that makes your heart so full you have to cry so you won't explode. That love has never left me. I miss Detroit every day.

People who transcend hesitation, especially when it comes to doing good deeds, are deeply comforting. We know they will help us if we need help. We won't need to talk about it. We won't need to ask. A year ago I went back to Detroit to visit Still Point Zen Buddhist Temple, a place that was my home for five years. These days I live on the wages of a part-time slightly-over-minimum-wage job. This meant that I left Seattle with forty dollars in my pocket to get me through the four-day trip. Planning ahead, I had packed my duffel bag with nuts, dried apples, and granola bars. They would be my meals. I already had places to stay.

The forty dollars was gone by day two. Water for the airplane, a big tip for the shuttle driver who went out of his way to get me to the airport on time (may he never drive that fast again), the need for aspirin and toothpaste when I landed. By the time I got to Still Point I was down to eight dollars with three days to go. In the middle of my visit, surrounded by people greeting me, one of the Guiding

Teacher's best friends, Charlie, came up to me and put an envelope in my hand. I put it in my pocket, figuring it was a note asking me to chant for someone. I get lots of those.

When I finally pulled the envelope out and opened it, two hundred dollars in twenties waved hello. They paid for lunches for three friends, a much-needed haircut, and another big tip for the same shuttle driver, who, it turns out, just likes to speed.

I don't even know Charlie.

It didn't matter.

My friend David has the same tendencies. He is forever stepping into a situation to help before the rest of us have even registered that a problem exists. A classic David story happened at a bank in Ann Arbor, Michigan.

His mother had sent him a sizable check to buy a certificate of deposit for her. He got her check on a Friday afternoon and planned to deposit it the following week. A phone call from his mother changed his plans.

"Go deposit the check now."

Ever the good son, he did. It was 5:30 p.m.

When he got to the bank, he overheard a woman upset about a deposit that hadn't been made into her account. She needed money to rent an apartment the next day. The bank couldn't help. David loaned her a thousand dollars on the spot. A complete stranger. David and Charlie are the kind of people who prove to me, every day, that people are good. By leaning in to a situation and helping out, they hold up the world, these men.

ant to be around people who transcend hesitation. We buy their books. We want their art. We marry them when we can. For me, one of the most surprising paintings in Boston's Museum of Fine Arts is a portrait of a buxom woman with bright yellow hair and neon green eyes. The painting shouts at you. Thick, fast strokes of bright, bright colors. Looking at it, you can literally feel the energy it took to create the painting. It grabs you and won't let go, the way a poet grabs you when she reads the first poem she has written in a while—the one that made her burst into tears when she put her pen down, there was so much energy in it, the one that takes your own breath away as she reads it to you. In the Boston painting the woman is sitting in a chair, holding the rope of a baby cradle in her hand. You can't see the cradle. Behind her flowers with yellow centers fill a wall, not in any particular order. Red-dotted green circles fill the background behind the flowers. Somehow the painting is magnificent. Broad, strong brushstrokes and the outlines around the woman's body and chair told me it was a van Gogh.

Lullaby: Madame Augustine Roulin Rocking a Cradle was painted in 1889, a little over a century ago. It has the intensity of fearlessness. While I was at first drawn to Madame's eyes, what stayed with me were the flowers that popped off the wall. Van Gogh loved flowers. He grew up surrounded by gardens. Given the tragedies of his adult life, I suspect they were one of the reasons he was able to keep some grip on reality into his thirties. His father's parsonage with its walled garden at Nuenen in Holland was a lifelong source of inspiration for the painter. Van Gogh needed nature in his life. When he worked as an art dealer in London as a young man, he planted a garden in the yard of his little rental home. Poppies. Sweet peas. Mignonette. He visited gardens whenever he could, loving their clean energy and sheer beauty. He painted them without hesitation. You can feel his great energy on the canvases. Sunflowers. Irises. Paintings of gardens that would sell for millions of dollars after his death. His *Garden of Flowers,* sketched in 1888, recently changed hands for $8.4 million. *Irises,* a painting I've seen on everything from calendars to pot holders, has sold for $5.4 million. *Vase with Sunflowers* most recently sold for $39 million. It is the energy of the paintings, the emotion, the leaving-nothing-behind aspect of each one of his paintings that makes you either want to own a van Gogh or paint like he painted. He puts everything he has, and everything he is, into each brush-stroke. This is what transcending hesitation feels like.

Biographies of van Gogh say that when he lived in Provence, he was awed by its beauty. When he moved to Arles for two years, he surrounded himself with gardens. Poppies. Cutting gardens with their yellow marigolds, blue nigellas, and red zinnias. He loved the public garden facing his house and used it to learn how to paint different foliages and textures.

When van Gogh's on-again, off-again friend Gauguin came to visit him from Paris, Vincent painted still lifes of sunflowers to brighten the walls of their rooms. Although this effort did not protect them from having huge fights or van Gogh falling into mental exhaustion, it demonstrates his love for nature's beauty and his ability to throw himself into his work. One of their fights was so bad that van Gogh threatened his friend with a razor, and when Gauguin left he cut off a part of his own ear in an act of pure insanity.

When his brother Theo showed up to take him to a hospital, van Gogh threw himself into painting the hospital's courtyard filled with flowers and plants. It gave him some peace. In letters to his sister, the painter offered detailed descriptions of the plants and flowers he loved the best. Forget-me-nots. Roses. Daisies. Oleander. Anemones. Even as he battled overwhelming depression, he was able to see the beauty surrounding him and to appreciate its power to offer respite.

And even as his illness drove him into the Asylum of Saint Paul in Saint-Rémy-de-Provence, van Gogh continued to paint with great energy. Irises. Calendulas. Close-ups of sedges and oat grasses.

> *There once was a man who went to church one day and asked:* *"Can it be that my zeal has deceived me, that I have taken the* *wrong road, and have not planned it well? Oh! If I might be* *freed from this uncertainty, and might have the firm conviction* *that I shall conquer and succeed in the end." And then a voice* *answered him: "And if you knew that for certain, what shall* *you do then? Act now as if you knew that for certain, and you* *will not be confounded." (Vincent van Gogh,* Dear Theo: The Autobiography of Vincent van Gogh, *ed. Irving Stone* *[Garden City, NY: Doubleday, 1937], 28)*

When van Gogh died at the young age of thirty-seven, he left behind a legacy of energy in the form of more than 2,100 drawings and paintings he had done during the ten-year span that was his painting life. He threw all of his senses into his work. In one of his many letters to Theo, van Gogh described how he got his ideas. The trick, he said, was direct contact. To really immerse ourselves in whatever situation we are in without holding back. There, creativity could be found. And, at least while we are creating, peace. The world continues to honor his ability to transcend hesitation, making him one of the most revered artists in history.

Yes. You and I are surrounded by beauty. We have all the energy we will ever need waiting to be tapped. We don't have to go anywhere else. A nearby garden offers us the world. A plane trip can take us on a wild, unpredictable adventure. A new puppy offers us requited love. A new friend, a mirror. Why do we wait? The sooner we jump, the sooner happiness has a chance to sneak into our system.

three

Preparing the Ground: Clear Seeing

*I often wonder why gardeners shy away from petunias, the single best
annual for sunny places…. Certainly the petunia comes in enough
colors, shapes and habits to deserve special interest….*

—Henry Mitchell, *One Man's Garden*

Rich Tennant is a cartoonist who knows gardens. One of his best
cartoons shows a woman in a baseball cap overlooking her
garden. It is filled with men dressed in suits and ties. The caption:
"It was worse than Sarah thought—her garden had become infested
with worms, maggots, and personal injury attorneys."

Clearly she hadn't planned well. And she hadn't been watching.
Planning clarifies our intentions. I'm not talking about big plans.
Simple to-do lists work just fine. To do lists of things we want to
remember. This works for gardens, and it works for the larger issues
of our lives.

For example, if we want to start living a happier life, a powerful exercise is to simply make a list of the people in our lives who help us feel good about ourselves and then a list of those who don't. We can think hard about how to compassionately (for us and them) move the "don'ts" farther away from where we live, in terms of both distance and time. This is not rocket science.

Gardening has taught me how powerful such lists can be. It has taught me to respect planning in a way that I never did before. It has taught me how important it is to see everything clearly when I start. And to admit what I see. Gardens have taught me that when I simply undertake the next obvious task, miracles happen if I keep going. Happily, I've had a variety of teachers who back me up here. The youngest is a twentysomething gardener I met at the nursery. He didn't look like a gardener exactly. His bleached blond hair was spiked. He had a tattoo wrapped around his neck. I never got close enough to see what it said. He dressed in old T-shirts, mostly black, with old Doc Marten–looking boots. He had chains. He gave me some of the best advice I ever got from anyone.

One morning he showed up needing white flowers. Only white flowers, he told me. That can be hard to do. He rejected any flowers and plants I found for him that were mostly white but had an edge of another color. It took us hours to find all he needed to fill the backyard of a nearby estate. While we were looking I asked him what was the best advice he ever got about gardening. It was from his father. "You plant your seeds. Then you pull your weeds. That's about it." He added that he had learned that keeping plants properly watered was harder than people knew and that it was really important to trim plants that were blocking other plants. Mostly, though, he told me, "You need to see what the garden needs. The more time you spend in it, the more you'll see." And off he went with a truck-load of phlox, a pile of pale echinacea plants (I swear they had yellow in them. Since we had been hunting for over an hour by then, he was ignoring that, I think), and ground covers.

The best gardens, the ones that make us say, "ooh-la-la" to ourselves when we see them, are the result of seven simple things:

1. A vision or intention
2. A plan that grows out of that vision
3. Dirt
4. Tools
5. The seeds or plants
6. The planting of those seeds and plants
7. The vigilant maintenance of same

Outdoor artwork, furniture, and fountains are the icing on the cake. Along the way, avid gardeners do research, like collecting enough catalogs to fill a spare bedroom or spending the month of January on the Internet looking at nursery sites. They take time to really study the gardening space in an effort to figure out the state their property is in. They may visit other gardens and spend time with other gardeners to get ideas and advice. Each of these things is a simple act, a small doing. Each shows clear thinking about what we need to do to get started, as well as clear seeing of what already exists. Collectively, our actions result in gardens that are lovely beyond words and much loved. When we take similar steps related to other aspects of our lives—our jobs, our relationships, our passions—we blossom. Our days become filled with meaningful, positive experiences. Our hearts expand. We want to be more helpful to others. We are happy.

In Seattle there are a handful of places everyone knows—Pike Place, the Space Needle, where to catch the ferry to Bainbridge Island. If you are a gardener, you know the nursery where I work. It is a heaven-on-earth sort of place, filled with top-quality plants and trees and just about every garden-related product you can imagine.

The nursery was started in 1956 by a northern European couple whose business evolved from a wholesale shop to a destination point for travelers from Canada to Florida. All two acres of the nursery's retail space are crammed full of color and beauty and good-natured staff willing to go the distance for everyone who walks through the door.

It took me about a day to realize that my in-depth knowledge of cantaloupes wasn't going to carry me far. I was surrounded by master gardeners and long-term staff who threw genus and species names around as though everybody talks that way. It was pretty clear to them, somewhere around minute fifteen, that I didn't know my rear end from a wheelbarrow, so I was put in charge of the petunias.

It didn't take me long to figure out the four or five types, the regular old-fashioned petunias, the double ones, the vinelike ones, the ones that grow so fast they'll engulf your pet if you look away too long. Large petunias, grandifloras, can be up to five inches across with ruffled or fringed petals. Smaller varieties, multifloras, tend to produce more flowers to a plant. Both come in all sorts of colors. Through hybridization you can now find all kinds of multicolored petunias.

If you ask me, petunias are way underrated. Sort of like a middle kid who never causes any trouble, they grow, they flower like crazy, they flower some more, then they die, without the need for more than casual watering. They can be breathtakingly beautiful and are perfect for adding color to all green gardens. Best of all, even beginners have to work hard to kill a petunia.

When petunias were introduced from South America to Europeans in the nineteenth century, the Brits went nuts over them. In 1834 a famous gardener named John London called petunias the most splendid ornaments of the flower gardener. One Victorian gardener is said to have made a petunia bed twenty-one feet in diameter just to make sure he could see them from far away.

Every spring the nursery has thousands and thousands of petunias for sale. Sometimes they take up six massive tables. I'm talking about a sea of petunias. And yet, while I was the petunia lady, every day at least one person would walk up to me standing alongside this sea and ask me to direct them to the petunias. The first few times I would smile, step aside, and with a sweep of my arm show them all the choices they had before them. After a while, though, I started to feel uncomfortable at how few of us see what is right in front of us. I know I don't. A most frequent response to my radioed questions to the rest of the garden team about the whereabouts of a plant was, "Look down." Invariably the plant, flower, or shrub would be right there grinning up at me.

Clear seeing is everything in life and in gardening. The best gardeners notice yard problems even as they plan, and if they don't catch the problems then, they take care to minimize them before they spread. Nothing is ignored. I can't help but wonder how many of the other problems in our lives would exist if we were as careful. My guess is not many.

Like people, every plant has different needs. This is not something our teachers taught us when they sent us home with our cantaloupe seeds. For me, this meant that I assumed all plants and trees could thrive in a sunny, semiarid climate once I threw their seeds onto the ground.

So, so wrong.

Before we do anything like start a garden, plan a house, or begin a relationship, it helps to really see what we're dealing with. What are the truths of our lives right now? With plants this means paying closer attention to the climate we live in. (It makes a difference to people, too. I love living in an area with an inordinate amount of rain. I must have duck genes. I have friends who can't last here for more than a few months. Likewise, a string of perfectly sunny seventy-degree days makes me crazy.) How hot does it really get where you live? For how long? How cold? We think we know, but often we don't. I thought I knew until I got out a calendar and started writing down daily temperatures and rainfall amounts. It turns out that the climate I live in, famed for its constant rain, is much sunnier than any of us give it credit for being.

This one piece of knowledge can make the difference between a healthy garden and no garden at all. In the same way, watching our own moods—using a calendar helps—can tell us in a nonemotional way which days we should save for simply locking ourselves in a room with no cell phone and computer so we can do no harm. These are the give-in-to-chocolate-for-three-meals days, the ones where we would be insane to negotiate allowances, job changes, use of the family car, or sex. For example, when I was married I thought I was pretty even-keeled until my husband casually mentioned that I asked him for a divorce on every full moon.

Not believing him, I started tracking my moods on a calendar, and I'll be damned if the man wasn't right.

Since seeing clearly matters, I've just given you a perfect excuse for nosing around your neighbors' gardens and nearby botanical gardens, not to mention the landscaping around local banks and real estate offices, to see what everyone else is managing to grow success-fully where you live. "Go gape" is my unasked-for advice. If you are anything like me, you'll double your plant knowledge by the day.

You'll discover, the way I did, that plants that are native to your area survive best and usually look the best. It is the nature of survivors.

Given that we are already paying good money for small bottles of water, it is probably safe to assume that water will continue to be more expensive, and possibly less available, as we all age. This means that grass lawns are likely to become a thing of the past, given their greed for water. Happily, ground covers and perennials exist that are both lovely and capable of growing and thriving on less water. These are the native plants you want to consider. For example, in the rainy Northwest (where our dirt is really clay—not that we would admit this to anyone who lives outside the region), there are hundreds, maybe more, of natives that can fill a garden to any yard owner's content, beginning with the Rocky Mountain maple and ending with western columbine. As you gain experience spying on your neighbors' yards, you start to notice shrubs that are used over and over and ground covers that seem to merge where one yard ends and another begins. Take photographs if you won't get arrested. Then you can go home and decide where you want them in your yard, knowing that there is a high probability that they will thrive, even if you are a beginner.

Also, it is good to know our soil's personality before we put any-thing into it. Soil tests are cheap and can be found in the "impulse buying" section of any self-respecting nursery. Even though it's a pain to do, with no quick rewards, getting your dirt into shape may be the single most important thing you can do for your garden.

It's the same with people. Skillful parenting, for example, starts with clear seeing. What do our children really need, as opposed to what we think they need? If we pay close attention, we will see. As is true with our gardens, the rewards of constant skillful parenting may not show up until our children are fully grown. My mother is the single most ethical person I have had the good luck to know. When we were kids she drilled us in sharing, in telling the truth, in being responsible. We had chores. Big chores. Even at five I knew how to wash dishes, and did. I could clean a bathroom, fold clothes, boil milk for my sister's bottle. By twelve I could run a whole household. Sometimes I did.

If I broke something I paid for it, even if it meant a summer of doing odd jobs for neighbors. The summer I scratched "I love Randy" with a stick into the dirt on his parents' car, aided and abetted, not to mention cheered on, by his brother, John, I spent the entire summer doing jobs to pay for a new paint job. Who knew the stick would scratch the paint as well? I raked, mowed, babysat, and cleaned windows until I had the money. I think John's mom felt sorry for me because she gave me the most jobs.

I was nine.

Being raised in this way meant that I needed few rules as a teenager. Unlike my friends, I was curfew free. At the age of sixteen I could stay out until 3:00 a.m. if it took that long to get a train home from downtown Sydney. The only thing my mother ever said, as I walked out the door, miniskirted and made up to just this side of superslut, was, "I trust you to be responsible."

And I was.

Not once did I get into trouble, even though every weekend gave me lots of chances since I was running with an edgy crowd. There were drugs. There was alcohol. I stayed responsible, much to the disbelief of anyone who didn't know how I was raised. My mother had given me the nutrients I needed. And it didn't hurt to believe that my father would kill me, possibly literally, if I screwed up.

When we look clearly we notice that people need nutrients. Gardens need nutrients. The irony for us is that the best nutrients can come from shit. A lover leaves us. Downright shitty. But the lessons we learn are invaluable. We grow from these nutrients, this fertilizer. We learn what we really need in our lives instead of what everyone else, from magazines to reality television, tells us we need. We learn that we can survive pretty much anything that life throws at us, even death. Fertilizer does that.

When I spent my first summer at the Ann Arbor Zen Buddhist Temple, I rarely saw my dharma sister Haju jump up and down with excitement. I was always all over the emotional map—thrilled about a strong retreat just finished, sad about someone leaving the spiritual community without warning. Haju, by contrast, took everything in stride, except for one thing.

The day the manure arrived for our vegetable garden was a perfect summer day. That day she was up and at it early, clearing a huge space just behind our one tree next to the gravel driveway.

Then a truck so smelly that you could tell it was closing in on us a block away appeared. Haju was as happy as one monk can be. Even her eyes danced. And when the truck dumped what looked and smelled like a ton of horseshit in the clearing, she was immediately on it, mixing compost and shoveling the mountain onto the garden.

Oh, how the garden grew after that! Huge tomatoes by the basket. Kale to last an entire winter. Sunflowers over eight feet tall. Peppers to beat the band.

If you find yourself anywhere near horses or cows, you are one lucky gardener. Get whatever manure you can, and mix it up with an equal amount of compost until what you have in front of you looks suspiciously like soil. Compost isn't fancy. It can be obvious stuff like grass clippings and leaves, as well as not-so-obvious coffee grounds, tea leaves, crushed eggshells, and fruit pulp.

Mix your concoction with dirt, and cover everything you can— ground wise—with one to three inches of what you have, and watch the miracles start to happen. Get a cookbook that has a lot of recipes for tomatoes, peppers, onions, herbs, and kale because you'll be eating tons of these.

Seeing clearly means seeing what already exists in front of our faces before we start changing anything in our lives, in our yards, or on our porches. In gardening this means getting to know the shrubs, trees, plants, and hidden things like bulbs that are already home-steading on our land before we start adding anything. Hopefully you'll want to keep the things that already call your yard home. If not, good karma comes from at least trying to find a good home for the things you don't want. Putting them near a curb with a "Free" sign can do wonders. I've even seen half-alive trees hauled away. What about the plants that don't look so good? When a customer asked a landscaper friend of mine what to do about a dying plant she said, "Let it die." Harsh but sane. It is difficult to bring a dying plant back to life. It's not like we can give them mouth-to-mouth resuscitation, although I've tried.

Although this is a hard-won lesson, it is one worth learning. When things are dead, they are dead. A relationship. A job. A friendship. A flower. Orchids taught me this lesson of letting go. I cannot imagine a flower more beautiful than an orchid. Delicate, beautiful, sensual. Hued in every color from the most iridescent white to the deepest violet. The orchid family is one of the largest, maybe the largest, in the plant kingdom. There are more than thirty thousand varieties. The species are all over the place visually: "One species looks just like a German shepherd dog with its tongue sticking out. One species looks like an onion, one looks like an octopus. One looks like a human nose. One looks like the kind of fancy shoes that a king might wear. One looks like Mickey Mouse" (Susan Orlean, *The Orchid Thief* [New York: Random House, 1998], 43).

Some orchids grow in the branches of trees in jungles while others grow in loose soil in crevices on tropical islands. Some, epiphytes, seem to grow in the air. One would think that caring for orchids would be simple, given their near independence from every-thing around them. Water when dry, one would think.

Not so. Orchids only need food every two weeks. And they need so much humidity that virtually all the successful orchid growers I know—both of them—buy gravel dishes to fill with water for pretty much every orchid they add to their collection. The orchid then sits in its pot on top of the dish.

And lives, unless it lands in my house.

For a while I fought my bad luck. I wouldn't give up. Instead, I invited myself to every orchid owner's house I could to study how they kept their plants alive. I was a clear-seeing machine.

The Orchid Thief started it. One of its main characters, John Laroche, loved orchids. Loved, loved, loved. Spurred on by his obses-sive, wacky love of the flowers, I bought one. It lived two weeks. I finished mourning it right about the time the movie *Adaptation* came out. Bought a second orchid. It died, too. So I went to my favorite bank teller, Chris. He raises orchids. Don't worry, he told me. They were picky orchids. Try again.

So I did. I bought a beautiful, tiny pink orchid reputed to be able to survive temperatures as low as fifty degrees at night. Two weeks later, dead.

I went back to Chris. He told me that his first dozen orchids died. "It takes a while" to see what they really need. My last orchid lasted almost three months. Then I fed it with fertilizer that wasn't orchid fertilizer because I was too lazy to go get the correct fertilizer.

Died. The next one: right-sized pot. Correct fertilizer. Gravel in a
dish filled with water. Pot set on dish.

Died.

So far I haven't gone back to Chris. I must have killed orchids in
a past life, I'm so good at it. At this rate, in my next life they will be
killing me. No need to push my luck, I tell myself. Dead is dead.
Time to move on.

Clear seeing, whether it is seeing what orchids really need or
seeing what needs cleaning up or nurturing in another aspect of our
lives, can be its own path to happiness. The more clearly we see, the
more colors and textures and tastes and smells appear before us. We
are able to quickly recognize what needs to be done in our lives,
from little things to packing up and moving without spending time
in that excruciating bardo of "whatever shall I do?" It helps to practice
clear seeing before we sink too much money into our gardening, or
into anything else, for that matter. The more we practice seeing clearly,
the more proficient we'll become. And I promise you that the more
proficient we are in seeing what is going on in one aspect of our
lives, the better we'll see what is happening elsewhere. Find a master
at clear seeing, and practice with him or her. Maybe it is a golf coach.
Maybe a Zen master. Maybe a painter.

Since I don't golf and my life is already slightly overflowing
with Zen masters, I study painters for pointers on clear seeing.
Gwen John tops my list. Born in England in 1876, John was Rodin's

model and muse as well as an artist in her own right. She attended art school in England when she was nineteen. Quickly tiring of the formalities of institutional learning, she decided to head for Paris, where Whistler tutored her for several months and where she found other artists to study with. Rodin became a huge influence. He demanded that she see clearly, not only through her practice of constant sketching but also by training herself to be well rounded through the study of philosophy, religion, and literature. For Rodin, learning about these topics was as important as understanding form, light, and color.

John has the ability to communicate the feeling, tone, and time of a place with very few brushstrokes and even fewer colors. She is perhaps best known for her paintings of a tiny attic room she lived in—pastel colors softening the austerity of the room. By the time she became Rodin's lover, she was well versed in many subjects and had committed herself to lifelong learning. It didn't hurt that she could talk about virtually any subject with his secretary, Rainer Maria Rilke. She discovered that by painting the same subject over and over, she was able to better discern nuances that were otherwise obscure. She filled her bookcase shelves with notebooks of sketches, focusing on a particular difficulty she was having, making sketches, writing comments, and noting advice she received from other artists.

Her pictures are quiet, almost mystical, in spite of the melodrama of her relationship with an openly philandering lover. She notices everything:

The light seems to change and change, from glinty green to
yellow gold to dove gray: there is a feeling of being secreted in
this ancient unspoiled land. Here is serenity, mystery, scope for
the imagination to run wild, and the freedom of somewhere
undisturbed.... In the contrasts of soft grey, yellow ochre, olive
green, and the dark Breton rocks there is visual magic. It
communicates itself powerfully in the tonal nuances.... (Gwen
John, quoted by Sue Roe, Gwen John: A Painter's Life *[New*
York: Farrar, Straus & Giroux, 2001], 183)

Or there is Giorgio Morandi. Born in Bologna, Italy, in 1890,
Morandi was the oldest of five children, lived well, and started out
his adulthood working in his father's business office.

He only lasted a year. He had to paint.

By 1907 Morandi was a card-carrying student at the Bologna
Academy of Fine Arts. Within a few years he was exhibiting and
earning some major prizes. He was mentally undone by World
War I and didn't do any better during World War II. When it was
over he literally retired with his mother and three sisters to an old
house on Via Fondazza, where he lived out the rest of his life. Like
Gwen John, Morandi needed the solitude and deep comfort of
working and sleeping in a single room. At one point, when asked
about his growing fame, Morandi replied that he didn't ask for
anything except for a bit of peace, which was indispensable for him
to work.

The artist loved shapes, colors, space, and light. He loved reality, seeing no need to explore further: "I don't think there's anything more surreal, or more abstract than reality," he said (interview for *The Voice of America,* recorded April 25, 1957).

When you look at his spare explorations of form and composition, the colors expand into new ones, and the shapes deepen. Through his clear seeing he gives us an opportunity to learn how to look. Copies of his paintings are the only pictures I have ever cut out of a book to hang on a wall. (Even though I own the book, I expect I'll still be going to book-destroyer's hell.) Simple paintings, they sing. They are happy. Nuanced. The subjects are ordinary: bottles, boxes, canisters, jugs, and vases. They always look like he found them in a bout of dumpster diving. Because he sees so clearly, he is able to paint the collections of his finds so exquisitely that women on the other side of the Atlantic are driven to cut copies of them right out of books. Okay, maybe it is just me, but still.

four

The Great Fertilizer: Generosity

This intention to benefit all beings,
Which does not arise in others even for their own sake,
Is an extraordinary jewel of the mind,
And its birth is an unprecedented wonder.
How can I fathom the depths
Of the goodness of this jewel of the mind,
The panacea that relieves the world of pain
And is the source of all its joy?

—Shantideva, *The Way of the Bodhisattva*

America's Second Harvest is a nationwide food bank network of over two hundred organizations that provide emergency food assistance to families and individuals across the country. Its goal is to end hunger in the United States. A local member of America's Second Harvest, Food Lifeline distributes 21 million pounds of food to hungry people each year. Their belief is that enough surplus food exists in the Northwest to feed every hungry person in western Washington; the issue is how to get it to them. Working with farmers, grocery stores, restaurants, hotels, and corporate kitchens like Microsoft's, the organization feeds over 500,000 people every year. Almost half are children. They do this by distributing the food they get to 250 food banks, meal programs, and shelters in seventeen counties that start at Washington's northernmost border and end at the Oregon line.

They could feed another 400,000 if they had the resources. The need exists. I'm not talking just about families who need welfare or are caught between jobs. Most of the families and individuals who get food work for a living. Take Anne, for instance: "My own experience is that I hold a job. I have a home. I'm not living on the streets. I'm not on any sort of federal assistance. I don't qualify for assistance because I make $200 a week. It's very hard to live. I think people might be [thinking], 'Why don't they get a job?' I do have one" (*Food Lifeline Accountability Report,* 2005).

I get this. Working at a nursery for slightly more than minimum wage, I can't comprehend how people with families survive. If I had one more mouth to feed, I'd go under.

Dharma Sound Zen Center community members volunteer at the distribution center two or three times a year. On my first day as a volunteer, our job is to pack grocery bags full of food for a holiday drive. QFC, a grocery chain that has been deeply generous to Food

Line, is making the drive possible. This is how the drive will work: Regular QFC customers will buy a bag of groceries for ten dollars. Each bag contains:

- A big jar of peanut butter
- 2 cans of fruit salad
- 2 cans of tuna fish
- 1 big container of oatmeal
- 2 big cans of tomatoes
- 3 boxes of macaroni and cheese
- 2 packages of spaghetti

About thirteen pounds of food in all. Once purchased, the bags will go to food banks across the region. The customer who buys a bag feels good because the food is worth way more than ten dollars. The food banks are happy because the food is well packaged, has a shelf life, and is nutritious. Food bank clients are happy because protein, especially, can be hard to come by when you are on a limited budget. Carbohydrates come cheap. Everything else doesn't.

Twenty of us are volunteering on a perfect fall Saturday. It may be the last sunny day of the season. Each of us has decided this work matters enough to give up the outdoors. It turns out that three different organizations are represented by us. In addition to the Zen Center, there is a Hindu youth group and a local bank.

We are divided into four groups, lined up at four tables next to a huge conveyor belt. The food is spread out in front of us. It is hard

not to feel like we are in a contest of some sort. Facing me at my
table are two young Hindus. Next to me is another woman from the
center. My job is the hardest. I have to make sure that all of the
correct food is in the bag, in the correct amounts, then line it all up
into a box shape, fold the top of the bag over, and staple a sign on it
that explains the program to grocery store customers. The woman
managing us can't overemphasize the need for neatness. People
won't buy messy or wrinkled bags, she tells us.

As soon as I have filled and stapled three bags, I put them in a box
on the conveyor belt. If they aren't perfectly lined up, they won't fit. I
feel like I'm in a television sitcom, so many things can go wrong. And
they do. I get behind because I can't get a macaroni-and-cheese box
lined up in a bag, and when I look up I'm surrounded by more bags
that need my attention. The bottom of a bag falls out. We run out of
tomatoes. Everything that happens is met with good cheer. I wish this
cheerfulness were available for more of us in our "real" jobs.

The pattern of the tables is this: Hindu/Buddhist, then the
bankers, then a table of Buddhists, then more bankers. You can tell
which is which from the conversations. Our table is quiet. We just
work and smile at each other when our eyes catch. The table behind
us chatters away—about sports, the Seahawks, bank politics, leader-
ship, and more sports. One of the members, a tall young man, is very
funny, a natural-born leader. Every once in a while the whole room
is chuckling at something he says—like telling a young Indian
woman beside him that she's a great "utility player." When she clearly

has no idea what he is talking about, he says, "You know, like in baseball. You can do every job really well." He is flirting, but because she doesn't understand the metaphor, even with the explanation, she misses it.

Each table finds its rhythm. At my table a young man in a red T-shirt printed with a Nike logo not only keeps up with the rest of us, he keeps us in supplies as well. Boxes. Food. Staples. When he sees me fall behind, without a word he comes to stand next to me to fold and staple until I'm caught up. Then he goes back to putting tomatoes, peanut butter, fruit salad, and tuna in bags.

Finally, we all run out of food to pack. As we leave, the young coordinator tells us that we packed 820 bags of food. We were fast. By her estimate that translates into over 10,000 pounds of food ready to go out the door. She wants to pack another 15,000 bags in the next two weeks and asks if she can e-mail us about additional volunteer dates. We nod yes and go home happy.

As part of my training to be a Zen teacher, eight years ago I shaved my head and went on a pilgrimage to South Korea. As is true with pilgrimages, the trip was nothing I expected. Instead of quiet cups of tea and gourmet vegetarian dinners followed by intimate chats with Zen masters, the four of us traveling together climbed mountains in sneakers, using public transportation when we could, mostly during a typhoon. Instead of incense, the smell I lived with was my own sweat. Instead of gifts, we got instructions.

At least they were heart filled. The one I best remember happened when a former monk came up to me as I was standing in the doorway of his house, readying my hot, exhausted, sweat-covered body for the next hike. He came so close to me that I was sure he was going to kiss me.

Instead he almost shouted: "Be like Samantabhadra!" He was giving me my life instructions and wanted to make sure I heard him loud and clear.

I did.

At the time I knew Samantabhadra only as one of the bodhisattvas or Buddhist saints whose name occasionally shows up in the old sutras. Because the monk was so insistent, and because I was so relieved that he didn't kiss me, I looked the saint up when I got home.

Samantabhadra is terrific. He is the embodiment of a deep generosity. In pictures and as a statue he is usually sitting on a lotus blossom, which is on a six-tusked, seven-legged snow-white elephant. Samantabhadra always looks happy and is amazingly calm given the implied bumpiness of his ride. Slightly smiling, he might be carrying a scroll, a wish-fulfilling jewel, a sword, or a teaching staff. The elephant is also always happy. He is either grinning from ear to ear or obviously laughing.

Samantabhadra vowed to be generous in particular ways—to confess his own misdeeds so someone else wouldn't get blamed for his screwups, to rejoice (rejoice!) in the happiness of others, to make offerings to everyone. The offerings could be big or small. It didn't matter. What matters is the spirit of the offering. So a little girl giving a monk a cookie is equal to the building of a school by a wealthy person.

We all get to be generous in whatever way we can without punishing ourselves for the smallness of what we are able to share. It all matters.

There is a Buddhist story about a king who lived in the third century, Ashoka, who was so generous that his ministers called a special meeting to tell him he had to stop because he had managed to give his entire kingdom away. He was so broke that when a monk walked past him, all he could offer the man was a partially eaten mango. The punch line of the story is that this act of generosity is the one that guaranteed his future as a Buddha, as much as giving away money, buildings, and land. The main teaching is to be generous however we can.

When we look, we see generosity everywhere. It is one of the forms of good news that doesn't get much media play. Victor's Celtic Coffee Company is easy to miss. It is on the wrong end of an alleyway, just off Redmond Way, a one-way street in Redmond, Washington. There are only about fifteen tables in the tiny, low-ceilinged spot. The place smells of plaster, wood, and rain, and the walls are covered with paintings done by local artists. Some are quite good. Some only a mother could love. Victor's entire back wall is papered with posters announcing everything from plays to parties and fund-raisers.

Even though Victor won't accept credit cards, an odd policy in an era when a credit card equals cash, the place is always packed. Word on the street is that Microsoft-related deals are done here every day. Big ones. Maybe. It is hard to tell since everyone in the place has the same logger-in-fitted-clothing look. On a morning when I decide I need coffee to survive, I sit next to a group of twenty-somethings working through a strategic plan. Across from them is a young mother with a little girl, maybe three. Her pink raincoat matches her polka-dot rubber boots. She could be a magazine ad. Next to them a couple plays cards with an old-fashioned card deck. They could be in 1955. Behind me a young woman asks her tablemate how long he has been at Microsoft. Nineteen months, he tells her. He likes it so far but doesn't think he'll stay much longer. He is homesick for Philadelphia.

The houses around the coffee shop are too expensive for most of us. Even the condominiums in Redmond require two-income house-holds or a Microsoft salary for mortgage payments. The entire city feels wealthy, young, and brash. Smart. The new town center is beautiful, like a miniature Disney World for shoppers. The library is as beautiful and as full of technology and books as any local library can be.

Bill Gates is the reason for all of it. Around here Gates is a super hero, not because he is richer than God, but because he has shared his great wealth with the world. By the end of 2006 Bill and his wife, Melinda, had given more than $30 billion away. Every week there is another story about his generosity. This morning I woke up to a news story announcing that their foundation is offering a $9 million grant to help local homeless families transition to independence. Included will be 140 housing units.

What amazes me about his story is that Bill Gates didn't start out as someone programmed to be one of the world's greatest philanthropists. It seems to have evolved out of his heart.

William Henry Gates III was born in Seattle on October 28, 1955. His mother was a schoolteacher, his father an attorney. As the myths around here tell it, Bill has always been a no-holding-back sort of fellow. In his senior year in high school, he and his friend Paul Allen, another rock-star philanthropist, built an entire computer by themselves. Later, as programmers for TRW, they wrote a program to help the company monitor electricity from dams—as their senior project!

In 1973 Gates headed for Harvard, where he mostly lived on hamburgers and pizza when he wasn't studying and writing computer programs. In 1974 Allen saw an article about an Altair 8800, the first affordable microcomputer. The two wrote a language for the company that made the machine and in 1975 folded all their efforts into a company they decided to start, called Microsoft. When they were able to sell their language to other companies, they became so successful that in 1976 Gates dropped out of Harvard to focus on the business.

The rest is history. He moved to Bellevue, a community across Lake Washington from Seattle. In the 1980s, when Microsoft made a deal with IBM to provide operating systems for their computers, they began to make money every time a computer was sold. Microsoft was on its way to greatness, and Bill Gates became a celebrity. By 1983 he was one of *People* magazine's twenty-five most intriguing people. By 1984 he was on the cover of *Time*.

Two years later the company moved east to Redmond. By 1987 Gates was the youngest self-made millionaire in history and Microsoft was the world's biggest software company. Gates could have rested on his laurels, but instead he started moving into the world of charitable giving, where he expects to put most of his energy, beginning in 2008. With his focus on health, poverty, and education, the world could not ask for a smarter, more skilled Samantabhadra.

Bill Kravinsky is someone else whose generosity takes my breath away. He is from Philadelphia and is clever enough to have made a fortune in real-estate brokering. When he was in his midforties he gave most of his money away. It added up to $45 million. Then he donated a kidney to a woman he didn't know. When he was interviewed about his gift of an organ, he said he would gladly give his other kidney to someone whose life was worth more than his. His rationale? The chances of dying from donating a kidney are about 1 in 4,000. For Kravinsky, not donating a kidney means that each of us is valuing our own life 4,000 times more than that of a person who needs a kidney. He was unwilling to undervalue someone else's life in such a way.

Big gifts like these change people's lives. So do small ones. Small doings. Many people in my life have very little money. Even though paying basic bills takes up most of their income, there is always room for generosity. My friend Daeja is a recently retired social worker from Detroit who now lives in a family-owned cabin in rural western Michigan. I don't think she has any income beyond social-services support. This doesn't stop her from sending me care packages of art supplies several times a year, supplies I would never buy myself. When I had to take time off because I wrecked my left foot at the nursery, a co-worker, Karie, showed up on my doorstep with enough food for a month. Yogurt, juice, cheese, crackers, soup, oatmeal, tea, beans, fruit salad, twenty-five pounds of puppy food. And socks. I spent her entire visit trying not to cry. It's not like she has any money, a car that works, or a bank account. She is Samantabhadra.

My neighbor Buster is moving. I casually mention to her that one of the gardeners I work with is in such bad shape that she is gleaning food and dumpster diving for furniture. The next thing I know Buster is leaving carloads of items by my door—blankets, towels, dishes, a bread maker. As I write this, she still hasn't stopped. I am so motivated by her generosity that I clear out my own closets, adding more carloads of goodies to the gleaner pile. There is so much stuff that I end up making three trips to a local thrift store that supports cancer victims. Cleaning things out, I remember how good it feels to get rid of the clutter of our lives. When we give it away it feels even better. Each gift is small, a small doing. Added up, they make a home for my friend and raise significant money for the nonprofit.

Generosity is everywhere.

It is 6:00 a.m. on a January morning in Michigan. The state has been hit by an ice storm. When I look out my hotel window, what I see takes my breath away. Every single thing has an inch of ice covering it—lights, streets, trees, poles, everything. The world is glazed in diamonds. It is so gorgeous I don't even cringe at the thought of the extra ten minutes it will take to scrape the layer off the car so I can drive it.

A television station is expecting me for an interview in a little over an hour. They want to talk about a book I've just written, *The Chocolate Cake Sutra*. It summarizes some teachings from a Mahayana Buddhist text, the Flower Ornament Sutra. I don't know yet that the producer thinks it is a cookbook.

Since I'm used to winter-weather driving on icy streets, it doesn't occur to me to call off the interview. Plus I'm too curious not to go. I want to nose around the station and watch everybody work. On my way, a transformer explodes right behind me. The whole sky lights up. Fireworks, I think. How odd.

When I get to the greenroom, a very small room where guests can watch the show before it is their turn in the newsroom, a young woman is there, shouting into her cell phone.

"This is my reputation here! Where *are* you!"

She doesn't acknowledge me when I walk in. She doesn't stop yelling. Finally, silence.

She looks at me. "My client is a personal trainer." (She says this looking at my thighs. I want to formally thank her here for refraining from saying he could help me.) "He is scheduled to be interviewed right before you."

She stands up to pace. Sits down. Stands up. If she weren't so angry she'd be beautiful, with her shoulder-length, honey-blond hair and natural spunkiness. She walks out into the hallway to call him again. Same words. Same anger. Finally she walks back into the room, plunks down on a couch, and looks at me.

"So what are you here for?"

I can tell I'm hard to place. I'm in a skirt and sweater and am pretty much makeup-free. My hair is a mass of cowlicks I've tried to brush out, with no luck. I could use some lip gloss.

I tell her I'm Buddhist and at the station to talk about a book.

"I've always been interested in Buddhism. What's the main teaching?"

"Only be kind. That's pretty much it."

She looks hard at me. I can feel the words registering. She nods, stands up, and walks out of the room to call her client again. This time, though, her tone is softer. When she comes back in, the show's producer pops his head in the door. He looks at me.

"Where's the cake?"

"Cake?"

"Cake."

The book isn't a cookbook, I tell him. And I didn't know I was supposed to bring a cake.

My interview is coming up fast.

"I'll get a cake."

It's the young woman. She tells us she knows where a bakery is and looks at the producer. He says, "I won't stop you."

She disappears. Twenty minutes later she is back with two exquisite chocolate cakes and a huge cheesecake, along with forks, knives, plates, and napkins. She tells me that she couldn't decide which one to buy so she bought all three. She won't take any money.

Minutes later, I'm sitting with a young newscaster who deftly dodges the whole cookbook question by reading an excerpt about the Reverend Martin Luther King Jr. It is MLK Day. She says kind things about the book. I am touched by her generosity, by both of these young women. Each one is the age of my daughter, Jamie. Like her they hold up the world one generous act at a time.

I leave the station staff the cakes, the cheesecake, and the book. Walking out of the building, I see the ice sparkling greetings to the day.

Gardeners are known for their generous natures. If we are skilled, our gardens are always overflowing. It is great fun to share what we don't need or want anymore. Almost every gardener I've ever visited has wanted me to take something home with me. My friend Jill Collman gives plants to as many as two dozen people a year—just because. When Cindi, jaimie, and I have to clean out plants as part of our spring and autumn cleanups, we try to remember who can use the healthy plants that happen to be in the wrong place at the wrong time. Another friend, Ango, probably gives me a plant a month. It is the gardener's way. We can't plant new seeds if we have no room.

The older I get, the more I realize that being Samantabhadra is mostly about our actions. My mother lives in a tiny basement apartment in a fast-eroding city in western Massachusetts. She is poor by anyone's measure. That hasn't stopped her from constantly doing good works. She teaches people to draw and paint, to play pool. She was a constant volunteer for the state's most recent gubernatorial campaign.

She teaches me that generosity has a lot to do with where and how we spend our time. So these days, while I may be one of the smallest donors that Amnesty International has, I am one of the organization's eager and prolific letter writers, committing to a hundred at a time. Handwritten. The great surprise is that I've discovered that it is impossible to:

- Feel sorry for myself
- Be cranky
- Eat too much sugar or white flour

when I'm busy writing. Maybe someday I'll be able to help a prisoner of conscience to go home to his or her family. Even the remote possibility that this might happen keeps me going.

As we start to see more clearly, we quickly notice people who are giving themselves up for someone else's good. Cindi and I are in Medina, Washington, finishing up an installation of a new garden. When it is completed, hopefully soon, it will be beautiful. Now it is just muddy. With the constant rain, we have to keep a close eye on the

new plants and trees. Already we have had to do some replanting, and
we pulled up some young bushes that just couldn't survive the deluge.

It is almost three o'clock in the afternoon. We are working fast
to finish before dark. The house's project manager shows up out of
the blue. He's what I was raised to describe as a good old boy, with
his jeans, flannel shirt, and boots. He looks like a cowboy. I'm pretty
sure that the only reason he isn't chewing tobacco is because a grade-
school teacher invited a man to visit the class and tell about losing
the bottom of his mouth to chewing tobacco.

He's always seemed a little gruff to me, this guy. All business.
Today, though, he starts talking about the flooding we are all still
facing. He and his wife saved all of their belongings by carrying
everything up to the second floor of their house. They barely made
it. His neighbors weren't so lucky. They lost pretty much everything.
When he went to check on them, they were piling four truckloads'
worth of soaked stuff into piles—total losses.

He took everything to the dump for them. Paid the twenty-
dollar dump fee each time. Didn't ask for the money back. They're
retired, he told us. They had just lost everything they owned.

Then he helped a young single mother with three kids. She lost
everything, too. Took her stuff to the dump. Paid the fees. Didn't ask
for the money.

Then he helped two more families. Same way.

When I was in the Zen Buddhist seminary, my teacher, Sunim,
perhaps the gruffest old Zen master on the planet, used to tell us a

great story about his teacher, another gruff old guy. He instructed Sunim to go outside, and when he spotted a Buddha, to come back to the monastery complex to report the sighting. Sunim went out into the mountains and down to the village in search of Buddhas and came home empty-handed. His teacher sent him back out. Every day he had to look for Buddhas, for holy people. For a long time, nothing.

Then one day he realized that everyone is Buddha. Everyone is holy. When he told his teacher this, the teacher was delighted.

Every one of us is a hero just waiting to happen. Our job is not to be fooled by the boots or the hair or the tattoos. Or the mud.

John Wood left Microsoft to give himself to the children of the world. Bill Gates aside, his choice, on its surface, is a surprising one. Microsoft feeds brain cells and brainy people. They are treated well, paid well, health-cared well.

John was an up-and-coming international marketing manager for the company. He loved what he did and was good at it. He had the stamina to work long hours, long days, long years:

I had adopted the commando lifestyle of a corporate warrior. Vacation was for people who were soft. Real players worked weekends, racked up hundreds of thousands of air miles and built mini-empires in the expanding global colossus called Microsoft. Complainers simply did not care about the company's future. (John Wood, Leaving Microsoft to Change

the World: An Entrepreneur's Odyssey to Educate the
World's Children *[New York: HarperCollins, 2006], 6)*

Everything changed when he went on a twenty-one-day trek in
the Himalayas. Nepal's illiteracy rate was 70 percent. A chance
meeting led him to a Nepalese school, where he heard himself
promising to find two or three hundred new books for the children.
What is amazing about John's story is not that he found the books
and moved on to greater heights, it is the reaction of the people
around him to his call for help. His father basically became a
volunteer staff person for an effort that grew from three hundred
books to adopting schools. Volunteers showed up as staff people.
Even his very first e-mail, asking for help finding a few hundred
books, led to thousands of donations. Thousands.

John's reaction: "Bold goals attract bold people.... If you ask people
to reach deep, to think creatively, and to produce extraordinary results,
they usually will. Too often in our modern world they are simply not
asked." In five years the organization he created built more libraries than
any other charity on the Asian continent. A million books were donated,
a thousand volunteer fund-raisers took place, and twenty-three hundred new libraries were motivating children and adults to learn the love
of reading. John never asked for permission to do this. He just dived in,
determined to make the world a better place. Samantabhadra.

Generosity. The Kirkland Food Bank is tucked away on a dead-
end street behind a mini-mall. The building, when you drive up to it,

looks tiny, like a small ranch house with a huge attached garage. It is surrounded by tall pines. The feeling is woodsy.

Inside, the building feels more like an accordion that has been pulled wide open. It goes on and on. One room for dry goods. One room with a huge freezer-refrigerator, big enough for a dozen people to stand inside it. One room for bread and baked goods.

We volunteers are a motley crew. It is impossible to distinguish us from the food bank clients, with our well-worn shoes, coats that could use a good washing, and faded jeans. Although a handful of volunteers are older women, most are young. One group is here from a local college. The rest are here to fulfill a court-ordered community service commitment.

As we line up to hand out food, I realize how hard this is going to be. It isn't that we don't want to be helpful. We do. Even the community service folks are a little excited about getting ready to hand out food. It's that the food we are about to give away is food that most of us—maybe all of us—can't afford.

The grocery stores around here are generous in the extreme. This season Trader Joe's has been over-the-top generous. We have cases of organic foods to give away—yogurts, cream cheeses, hummus, soy. I try not to think about what it would cost to buy the case of organic milk products in front of me. Hundreds of dollars, maybe. I can buy organic milk only as a special treat. Four gallons cost as much as my monthly electricity bill.

I've never bought the hummus or tempeh. It's always made more sense to get three frozen pizzas instead.

I can feel a slight withdrawal taking place inside of me. It is one thing to give away leftovers or things I don't want or need, but this is different. Then I remember the story of Ryokan, a monk who returned home one day to find a thief loading up his few belongings into a big bag. Ryokan's response was immediate. He stripped and gave the man his clothes. Later, when the thief was gone, the monk sighed, saying, "Poor fellow, I wish I could give him this beautiful moon."

When I first heard that story, I couldn't imagine feeling that way. I wrote it off, figuring that living in the mountains by yourself, praying constantly, was what it took. Then a friend of mine, Kay Caskey Gould, told me a story about one of her students. Kay is a bodhisattva in her own right. She started a bookstore in Ann Arbor, which she and her partner, Jim, use as a means for employing people who need to work. Family. Friends. Me when I had a shaved head, left over from my South Korean pilgrimage, that needed time to grow out.

She is also a gifted art teacher. My daughter and I took her class on drawing faces. The only class we missed was the one on noses. To this day we can both draw lovely faces except for a blank space where the nose should be.

Kay's student had faced some real heartbreaks in her life. To recover, at one point she decided to face her greatest fear head-on. It was that a man would break into her house in the middle of the night and kill her. What would she do? Her response stopped us all in our tracks. She would make him a perfect breakfast before he killed her—taking time to ensure that it was both beautiful and delicious. She spelled out every detail of the breakfast. Reading her words on paper, I wondered if she was Ryokan reborn.

When I remembered her, my mood shifted. Not only would I give away food, but I would give it away with a heart filled with gratitude for the opportunity. My job was to give away granola bars in boxes. I handed hundreds out, sometimes opening a box to give individual bars to cranky kids or tired parents.

Food bank clients come from every ethnic group and every age. In Kirkland, many of the clients are Russian. We also feed Latino families, Asian families, and people from the Pacific Islands. Elderly women and men. Lots and lots of children. Babies. Each one is honored. They get to choose what they want to take, by category of food—which meats, which milk products. Every family can fill at least one grocery cart a week, depending on the size of the family. Boxes of healthy food move out of the food bank—fresh fruits like pineapples, persimmons, and bananas. Vegetables. Cases of frozen chicken. Some frozen geese. Gourmet soups. One of the clients gives me detailed instructions for finding some frozen vegetarian soup that has been tucked away in the back of the freezer for him. Because it is the holiday season, someone has also donated hundreds of poinsettias and bouquets of Christmas flowers. These go fast.

By 2:00 p.m. it is all over. We clean up and set things out for the food bank's evening hours. As I leave, a man is yelling at the food-bank coordinator: "You do not welcome me here! I never feel welcome! Never!" She is being patient. Whenever he stops to catch his breath, she replies, "You are always welcome here." She is a broken record, repeating it over and over. I recognize the man. When he came through the line he had the walk of someone who was drunk—that side-to-side lurch. I noticed because he almost knocked over the boxes of granola bars before I caught his elbow and handed him some food. He never looked at me or my egg-handing-out partner as we handed him the milk and yogurt he pointed at.

I went up to the two of them. "I'm happy to speak with you," I say to the man. I sense he feels lonely. I can be company while the coordinator goes to get some of her work done. "No," he responds. "I just need a minute." He starts yelling again. The coordinator doesn't take her eyes off him, receiving his verbal blows without fighting back. Later, as I drive away, after almost everyone else is gone, I look back. She is still standing there hearing him out. "You are always welcome here." These practices can be such hard work sometimes. When I go home I put her name on my altar. It is my secret way of covering her back, of giving back some of her generosity. When I see her again she is still calm, patient, and generous. She is Samantabhadra in blue jeans and a ponytail.

We think we can't give our lives to something, but we can. Maybe we can give ourselves to the world for only a morning or a day or a week. When a friend of mine was ordained as a Zen Buddhist priest, to express her gratitude she went to India to work with Mother Teresa. It was heartbreaking, backbreaking work.

Problems were insurmountable. Every night she went to sleep knowing that some of the children she was working with would be dead the next morning. Looking back at her letters, I see a happy person—have rarely seen a happier one. She was giving the experience everything she had. Maybe she couldn't help all the children, but she could help some of them. She could help them put on a Christmas play and make ornaments. She could laugh with them. And clap.

Joy flies off the pages of her letters. This is what real generosity does. It transforms us down to our cells. From this place, eradicating poverty everywhere becomes possible. Forgiveness becomes a given, and faith in possibilities becomes our mantra.

five

Planting Like You Mean It: Enthusiasm

Yesterday I dreamt that a bullet went off
while we kissed
and neither of us let go of our hope.
This is a love
that belongs to no one.
We found it mislaid
shipwrecked
in the street.
Between you and me we retrieved it
and gave it shelter.

—Carilda Oliver Labra, "Eve's Discourse"

She has thick dark brown hair that almost reaches her shoulders. Until recently it was dreadlocked. Her uniform is a pair of cinnamon-colored short pants topped by a North Face rain jacket, gray and green. She wears riding boots. Clear skinned and clear eyed, she is both a chick magnet and a boy magnet. Her preference is chick. Practically everywhere we landscape together she is invited for coffee. It is her natural beauty. She glows from the inside out. I don't think she knows this.

Jaimie healy grew up in the public housing projects of North Philadelphia. Raised by a single mother, she made her way into art school and is presently making her way into the hearts of collectors. At her first Seattle show every painting sold, a laudable accomplishment for a twenty-nine-year-old.

Her specialty is crows. Black crows on off-white paper. Lots of versions. They are ethereal and lovely. To see their beauty is a shock to my system. It turns out that there are some forty-five species of crows. Sometimes they aren't called crows; they're called instead ravens or jackdaws or rooks. If you spend any time around them you'll notice that the birds refuse to be ignored. They sing, scold, and swoop, constantly and fearlessly. In some of the Native communities along the Northwest coast, crows are revered as a living tradition that imparts its irreverent and ribald spirit to the world at large. Since Seattle can be both irreverent and ribald, the crows do their work well around these parts.

I always knew that crows were smart. For their size, they are smarter than other birds and most mammals, with the possible exception of parrots. Crows know how to find food that has been hidden and how to pretend to hide food somewhere so it can be safe in its real spot. They can make tools out of leaves and carry the tools to feeding sites to help them pull food out of holes. They have even been observed keeping the tool and storing it for later use.

Mostly, though, crows are scavengers, nature's cleanup crew. I once heard someone describe them as having a diet that includes the dead and the rotten. Not something one would consider as a subject for paintings—unless you are jaimie.

The woman loves crows. She stops working to watch them, collects pictures of them, collects their skulls, and buries the dead ones we find. When she paints them, all of her permeates her work, making each piece strong and soft somehow, eye-catching and thought provoking.

What people love about jaimie is her enthusiasm. She always arrives on time, ready to work. When we figure out what tasks need to be done each day, she grabs the tough jobs first: climbing a fourteen-foot hedge to trim it; attacking a long hilly driveway with a leaf blower. Jaimie is quick to jump onto the back of the pickup truck to grab the tools any of us need and the day's tarps before it occurs to me that we'll need them. She is always smiling, even on the days when it is raining so hard we can barely see each other, even on the days when her head hurts. She doesn't stop working until the jobs are done.

Her energy is palpable. When we talk, which isn't very much, we tend to focus on gardening: why some plants last and others don't; whether we should cut down some bamboo that is overtaking the

entire south side of a house; what to do about a berry bush that is
too close to a door. We see how birdbaths have a way of seducing
birds into a yard, even with a lake a few feet away, and how shrubs
such as junipers, hollies, and cotoneasters act as natural bird havens.
We can attest to the fact that the feeders and bushes don't have a
chance if there are any cats or squirrels within, say, a mile radius.
And we've learned from our clients. How to plant dead-looking tea
roses in a container so they will spring back to life, or at least not die.
How to hang chimes to keep bees away from the parts of gardens
where children will be playing.

Jaimie notices mistakes that I make and simply takes care of
them without bothering to mention what she's done. I hope she'll
never leave gardening, knowing she will. Her artistic talent will pull
her away from us as she is discovered by more collectors. It is her
enthusiasm I'll miss the most.

In *The Way of the Bodhisattva*, Shantideva singles out enthusiasm as an attribute that feeds our happiness. Enthusiasm for the
work we need to do is a huge part of what he is talking about. As
someone who grew up bribing her little sisters to do her chores, this
has been a major "aha" of my adult life. Enthusiasm always brightens
a situation. It feeds energy. It feels good.

When I was a seminary student, my teacher demanded enthusiasm. He taught us that four things would feed it: wanting to be
enthusiastic; sticking with it; letting ourselves be happy; and being

careful not to get too carried away because that could lead to having-to-lie-on-the-floor exhaustion.

We had to choose enthusiasm, something that doesn't come naturally in a society that is already rushing us through our days. If we couldn't feel it immediately, we had to give it a little time to kick in. For most of us, especially those of us reared in the land of cynicism, this meant not judging ourselves, or him, too harshly too soon. Along the same line, we had to give ourselves permission to feel the joy that is a by-product of enthusiasm. Joy can be a little embarrassing if you aren't used to it. It feels a little too Hallmark TV Channelish. A little false. Except it isn't. It's true and it feeds our happiness, our health, and our sanity as it balances out the inevitable sorrows in our lives.

Sunim didn't want us to just lean in to whatever situation we found ourselves in, he wanted us to jump into it. When wake-up chanting started at 4:00 a.m., our job was to immediately get up, wash up, and quickly enter the meditation hall as though we couldn't bear to be outside it for a second longer. Ever the lazy sister, I balked at this for a long time. Finally it took too much energy to resist Sunim, so I started getting up quickly enough to enter the meditation hall before anyone else. It felt wonderful to arrive, heart pounding, water drying on my face. The effort meant that I was really awake when we started to do our formal spiritual practice. I never fell asleep while we were meditating, even on mornings following three or four hours of sleep. Because we were all enthusiastic, the temple was filled with a happy energy. The times when we raced each other to answer the doorbell were times when we would end up laughing uproariously, just because.

I can tell when people live their lives with enthusiasm. They are surrounded by things they love. They are happy. And they are helpful—whether you are an old friend or a stranger asking for directions. If they have gardens, large or small, the gardens are textured and interesting. Usually there is art somewhere in there, or a birdbath or chimes. Maybe there is a bench tucked away in a corner. Working in people's yards, I am constantly reminded of the beauty that is enthusiastic effort. I think of hummingbirds and butterflies. In the Northwest, hummingbirds are fairly common. They show up pretty much wherever bell-shaped flowers are grown. In the nursery we stop and stare whenever a hummingbird finds its way into the perennials. They are the bird equivalent of happy pills. Hummingbirds fly into a flower so fast and hard that I always think they'll fly right through the petals, although they never do. Then they hover with wings beating at the speed of light, twitching and eating and dancing their hummingbird dance, until suddenly, without pause, they zoom off to their next meal. Everyone caught up in watching them ends up smiling and even laughing with pleasure. I say each of us needs to lure them into our lives, whatever it takes.

Plants That Hummingbirds Love

- Agastache: Spikelike flowers that smell great.
- Hollyhock: Old-fashioned flowers to circle the bench in the corner.
- Delphinium: Great for at least two rounds of flowers in a season.
- Foxglove: Really tall and tubular, their stems can grow up to eight feet.
- Coral bells: Evergreens that can be tucked into rock gardens and used as ground cover. Oo-la-la.
- Lupine: Leaves spread out like fingers of a hand holding up flowers that look like little sweet peas.
- Crocosmia: Provides splashes of color that look like they will glow in the dark.
- Bee balm: Can grow to four feet tall. Smells like basil mixed with mint, and the flowers look like they have wild Halloween haircuts.
- Geraniums: Hard to kill. A good choice for beginners.
- Sage: Actually part of the mint family. Comes in just about every hue you can imagine. Another great-smelling plant.

Butterflies also live with great enthusiasm. Just try following one with your eyes to see what I mean. They always cheer up a garden. Butterflies love sun and flowers with nectar. That pretty much sums it up. I paid no attention to butterflies until I went to Costa Rica, where I met about a gazillion different varieties. Okay, not that many. The country is home to at least a thousand varieties. Frankly,

I got dizzy trying to keep count. After I found the butterflies that disguised themselves as everything from leaves to bird poop, I was hooked. Happily, Seattle has a butterfly garden in its zoo. While I have yet to make the acquaintance of the animals that live at the zoo, a summer isn't a summer without a visit to the hyperactive little insects living in two greenhouselike buildings that feel alive when you walk into them. The plants and flowers alone would be worth a visit. They fill the 3,900 square feet from end to end, offering almost every combination of trees, shrubs, and flowers that a butterfly could hope for. It feels like a little butterfly heaven. And while I haven't personally counted them (this doesn't mean I haven't tried), zoo staff say there are a thousand butterflies living in butterfly world at any one time. That the butterflies live only about two weeks always makes for a little sadness and a renewed gratitude for a life that is longer than two weeks. So far my favorite is the red-spotted purple or maybe the zebra longwing. Probably this is because, except for the monarchs (or was it a viceroy?), these are the only two I've spotted so far.

Ten Plants That Butterflies Love

- Snapdragons: Perfect for sunny borders and vases. Also fun to play with: by lightly pinching the sides of a flower you can make its jaws snap open. Just try to stop.
- Lavender: Worth growing for the smell alone. Lavender is great for hedges and edges.
- Nasturtium: One of the prettiest flowers on the face of the

planet. They grow fast and are incredibly easy to draw.

- Passion vine: The flowers are so beautiful they look fake. Each one has at least three colors. Great for trellises if you live in the right climate. If you don't and try to grow the plant anyway, your life will become bitter; better to find something else.

- Hibiscus: Comes in lots of forms—annual, perennial, evergreen, deciduous, shrubs, trees. Color possibilities range from white to bright (and I mean *bright*) red.

- Tree mallow: Easy-to-grow shrubs with old-fashioned, Victorian-looking flowers.

- Roses: You know what roses look like. I find them incredibly hard to keep alive, sort of like orchids. It must be my karma or something.

- Butterfly bush: I call it butterfly crack. If you put one in your yard, you will see what I mean. If it dies for some reason, expect to see butterflies protesting at your windows and upending your car.

- Hebes: A favorite garden filler with a huge choice of shapes, sizes, and colors. Hebes grow fast and are pretty durable, and many of them have lovely miniature flowers that work well in vases.

- Lantana: More butterfly crack. The flower clusters look like miniature nosegays and are adorable if you can find tiny vases for them. Lantana is so pretty that it is worth growing even if you don't care about the butterflies.

➤➤

Enthusiasm counts for a lot in life. My introduction to Carilda Oliver Labra was this: "There's this Cuban poet you should read. She has the energy of a teenager even though she is in her eighties." Labra was born in Matanzas, Cuba, in 1922. At Havana University she studied law in addition to taking classes in painting, drawing, and sculpture. She also studied poetry, writing her first book, *Preludo Lírico*, at twenty-one. Her voice is the voice of a woman who is fearless about being enthusiastic about her life, whether it is fighting corruption or falling in love with a much younger man. Her last lover and husband was almost forty years her junior. She also uses poetry as a weapon against war:

> *Please don't point your weapons*
> *at the sky:*
> *the sparrows are terrorized,*
> *and it's springtime,*
> *it's raining,*
> *the meadows are ruminating.*
> *Please, you'll melt the moon,*
> *only night-light of the poor.*
> *It's not that I'm afraid,*
> *or a coward.*
> *I'd do everything for my homeland;*
> *but don't argue so much over your nuclear missiles,*
> *because something horrible is happening*
> *and I haven't had time enough to love.*
>
> —"Declaration of Love"

For Labra, poetry is the manifestation of enthusiasm. It tells the truth. It praises beauty. It unites us in the fight against injustice. It captures the power of small moments, small actions, small doings. It kicks us in our collective rears, reminding us that life is bursting with beauty, love, and awe in spite of any and all heartbreak that could be waiting for us around the next corner. How can we not step into its arms?

Enthusiasm can make the difference between a life well lived and a counting-the-days-till-it-ends life. Back in my management-consulting days, one of its great pleasures was working with start-up entrepreneurs. Ever optimistic, they were invariably filled with energy and a contagious enthusiasm. The woman who wins the-most-enthusiastic-person-I-ever-met award wanted to start a company to help people meet their soul mates.

I was working for a nationally known conservative accounting firm. We didn't acknowledge the existence of soul mates. Plus, in Buddhism since there is no such thing as a permanent soul, even the term *soul mate* is a little problematic.

I helped her anyway. I helped her because her enthusiasm made a believer out of me. I helped her because her own enthusiasm had led her straight to the love of her life. And successful love stories always have something to teach the rest of us.

First the husband: good-looking by anyone's standards. Older, sexy, laugh crinkles around his eyes. Now her: not someone you would notice on the street. Glasses, not fashionable. Heavyset. Not even a nod to fashion. Support stockings. Practical pumps.

But there was her enthusiasm. It made her charming and sexy. Within minutes, I was enthralled with her. The story she told me only made me like her more.

When she was a teenager, the kind nobody notices and teachers don't remember, she decided to start writing love letters to her future husband. The first ones were pure teen, with hearts drawn everywhere on the paper and big, girly printing. When she was in her twenties, the letters were more newsy and loving. By her thirties, she was writing long letters filled with the details of her days. She put the letters in albums. In the meantime, she didn't date at all. I'm guessing nobody asked. Kathy was the kind of woman you fell in love with only if you found yourself in a room where there was just the two of you facing each other across a table.

Except for the enthusiasm. People noticed that. It was the reason I had agreed to meet with her for free even before I knew the purpose of her business. It was the reason for her success.

Anyway, as I remember it, she was closing in on forty and went to a Halloween party fully costumed as a cow. The costume included a cow's head and a tail. It looked like the kind of outfit a rich kid might wear to a kindergarten party, only this costume was adult sized. Midway through the party, as she leaned down to pick something up off the floor, she heard someone say, "I'd love to know what kind of person would have the guts to wear a full-blown cow costume."

It was her future husband. They instantly fell in love. He loved her energy, and the letters. He was exactly as she had pictured him.

Enthusiasm, action by action, feeds a life that is becoming a garden. Once we have a sense for where we are headed, the trick then becomes learning what is too fast and what is too slow. Too much enthusiasm is the path to burnout.

Working for over a dozen different families, I've learned that the most exquisite gardens were developed steadily—not all at once and not too slowly. A handful of plants, including shrubs and trees, were planted each year. This was a useful discovery. For a while it felt counterintuitive. When most of us start out on a new adventure, like a new garden, we want instant, or at least quick, rewards. A garden that looks full. A guitar that sounds mastered. The problem with gardens is that the ones that look mature at the end of the first year are often the ones that need road crews to cut them back five years later. Where I live, for example, cypress trees grow so fast that what new gardeners planted as a natural fence can permanently block the sun at twenty feet in about six years. Or the adorable Japanese maple that you buy at three feet and plant next to the front door grows into something so fat and round that either everything around it needs to be replanted somewhere else, or it does.

Finding out what is "just right" comes with that old favorite, clear seeing. We take the time to learn the growth habits of what we are buying. We watch our own energy to see when we shift from feeling happy when we wake up each morning to wishing it were Friday on a Tuesday. I once failed a koan interview, not because my response was incorrect, but because it was tentative. When I responded again, I was over the top. The teacher reminded me that my job was to live my life with 100 percent enthusiasm—not 70 percent because I would miss things that I needed to learn, but also not 110 percent because that would lead to an overgrown life, exhausting to me and everyone around me.

So our enthusiasm needs to be focused on the "just right," the level of effort that leaves us happy-tired, like a little kid after recess, instead of exhausted-tired, where it is all we can do to get to the couch to sit and stare. Happy-tired leads to more energy and a feeling of well-being. The other kind of tired? Burnout and a search for medicinal happy pills. As I thought about this, I realized that part of the delight of jaimie, soon-to-be-famous artist, and Kathy, finder of soul mates, is that they have "just right" down. Jaimie knows how to blow leaves to the edge of a driveway without pushing them over the neighbor's side bank. We plant three-foot maples instead of seven-foot ones. From her I've learned, for example, to keep a steady three-mile-an-hour pace on walks so I can actually see the flowers I might want to stop to smell. Every year I look forward to seeing the new shapes in client gardens, shapes that don't overwhelm what was already there. Every year the gardens become a brand-new experience, triggering ideas for the next season, and the next.

six

Weeds and More Weeds: Taming Our Minds

But if the elephant of my mind is firmly bound
On all sides by the rope of mindfulness,
All fears will cease to exist
And all virtues will come into my hand.
—Shantideva, *A Guide to the Bodhisattva's Way of Life*

The e-mail shows up on Sunday afternoon. Monday is going to be a hard workday. "The hedges need work. Be prepared with ladders and tools."

I fall asleep trying not to think about the next morning and fail. It has been pouring all day with forecasts of the same when we wake up. At least three of my dreams are about drowning. The woman on the radio announces, "One hundred percent chance of rain," when the alarm goes off at 5:00 a.m.

I try not to think about it. Still, I layer up. Three shirts. First the short-sleeved T-shirt. Then the long-sleeved cotton one. Then wool. Then three layers of pants. The top layer is rainproof. I am wearing so much clothing that I feel like that kid in *The Christmas Story* who falls down in the snow and can't get up. I know if I trip on anything it will be all over. I may never be upright again.

By 6:00 a.m. I am walking Bodhi through the park next door. If it weren't for the streetlights, it would be pitch-black. The rain is coming down so hard I can barely see Bodhi at the end of his leash. But I can feel him, happy and tugging. He loves the rain. It must be the Labrador half of his lineage.

When we walk past the neighborhood Starbucks, it is open but empty for once. It reminds me of Hopper's diners, all lit up with no one in sight. I've never seen an empty open Starbucks before. We stop to look in the windows. I can't help myself. It looks so warm and dry. I only start moving again when I see, out of the corner of my eye, Bodhi jumping into a puppy-sized lake where some leaves have clogged a drain. He is yelping with happiness.

We are both, by now, drenched. Rain has found its way into my cuffs, and the ground is so wet my socks have become a wick driving the moisture down into my rainproof shoes.

I don't mind. Mostly, I love rain. What I don't like, though, is climbing on ladders in high winds, trying to trim hedges with tools that weigh anywhere from fifteen to over forty pounds. Gas-filled hedge trimmers are unwieldy in the best of circumstances. As I think about the day facing me, I'm feeling more like Eeyore by the minute.

When Bodhi and I turn back toward home, it is 6:30 a.m. My mind is in full frenzied mode. Traffic is so jammed the cars are just sitting in a long, mostly patient (it is still early) line. I start obsessing about our ladders. They are aluminum. The good part is, I can carry one with one hand. The bad part is, wind can knock them over easily. The sitting cars tell me that even if I leave an hour and a half early I won't make it to work on time. On Monday mornings Seattle's rush hour can beat that of Los Angeles easily. Add rain, and we all have time to read a chapter in a favorite mystery novel between light changes.

I keep thinking about the rain and the wind. We can take turns on the ladder, I tell myself. I'll go first for an hour while jaimie holds the ladder. Then she can take a turn. She's much stronger than I am. She'll get a lot more trimming done. Then maybe Cindi will have a go. She's the strongest of the three of us, and she has the most experience. We can probably do the whole hedge in three turns. Not so bad.

The wind picks up as Bodhi and I turn into our building's garage. No, I think. It will be too dangerous. We should all just quit. This close to the holidays we'll all find jobs. A wind-free, dry workplace trumps coastal wind and rain any day. Or maybe we should just work for a couple of hours and take a long lunch, say two hours, dry out, and then work some more. That could work. The client will understand. No, my mind says. Just quit.

The trouble is (I'm now arguing with myself), I really love the work. And I love my gardening team. Christie is a fair boss. She pays us well.

We laugh a lot while we work. We talk books, culture, philosophy. Plus, organic landscaping is a terrific workout with or without rain.

Back home, I throw Bodhi into the tub for a quick shampoo since he is already halfway there. I dry him off and head for the shower. Dried, we are both happy. While the oatmeal cooks, I make a huge lunch to take with me. We'll get hungry. Two yogurts, four slices of cheese, a quarter of a loaf of French bread, an avocado, two bananas, and a chocolate bar. I'm planning to share.

My brain is still going back and forth about whether or not to even go. Shrugging, I put on a rain slicker. It is 7:45 a.m., a little late to start out. For sure I won't make it by 9:00 a.m. At least I'm dry and warm. I grab a book to read during the traffic stall-outs that are now being described in painful detail on the radio.

The phone rings. It is Christie. "No work today. It's too bad outside."

I've just wasted hours fussing about something that now will not happen.

Hilarious.

Weeds happen. They pop up in gardens, and they pop up in our minds in many forms. Random thoughts. Angry thoughts. Worried thoughts. Fantasies. They move like storm fronts through our brains. It seems you and I mostly don't mind the storm fronts, given their high levels of entertainment. They fill up our days just fine, thank you very much. Maxed out, they prove we are alive and filled with feelings. When I'm really angry about something, I feel powerful and energized. I have a battle to fight. When I think about a lost love, I can wallow in seductive melancholy for days. How could he have left? He'll never, ever find anyone like me! Or, just as painful: How could I have left? I'll never, ever find anyone like him again! It gives me an excuse to mope around, read lightweight romances that will remind me of how good it all was (not that my romance-related memories have anything to do with reality), and eat chocolate chip cookies to my broken heart's content.

It takes guts to admit we are fond of these storms of emotion. When we do have the courage, though, we can start unraveling what Shantideva calls *kleshas*, to free the less intense but potentially delightful experiences of compassion and wisdom lying just behind them. Some spiritual traditions call this phenomenon of emotional storm fronts and their aftermaths "monkey mind" because the brain chattering is so incessant. We swing from one thought to another, from one emotion to the next, without any breaks. The ancient language Pali calls this *papanca:*

> *The exact derivation of papanca is not entirely clear, but its*
> *sense hovers somewhere between the three nodes of:*
> *to spread out or proliferate*
> *an illusion or an obsession*
> *an obstacle or impediment.* (Buddhadharma *[Fall 2006], 82)*

Papanca is our tendency to take one experience—say, the need to work outside on a windy, rainy day—and to move out from there,

fantasizing about the things that might happen and letting in emotions that are related to these fantasies until we've landed in never-
never land. Most of this thinking not only is illusory, it also repeats
itself often enough to become obsession.

The downside of this phenomenon—one we all share—can be a
total loss of calmness, let alone clarity. Plus, even if there are some
rewards, like the excuse to eat too many pieces of chocolate cake
before 8:00 a.m., it can be exhausting. I know I was ready to go back
to bed after Christie's phone call.

When we start to notice our wild and crazy minds, we also start
to see just how much our thinking determines our levels of—let's just
call it what it is—sanity. When we know this, taming our thoughts
becomes an important task. The first step to this taming is simply
seeing what is going on up there in the first place. To pay attention,
meditation helps. So does gardening. Especially gardening tasks
where we really have to pay attention, like clearing blackberry bushes
on a steep hill or weeding beside a foundation for red ants.

Pretty much anything that forces us to really pay attention can
calm our monkey minds. Climbing rocks. Parasailing. Trimming
hedges in the wind.

Each of us can find our own way here. While meditation works
for me, my friend Roger prays. A nun friend chants constantly. Koho
and Bhaddaka climb rocks, cliffs, walls, and abandoned train stations.
Neil makes music. Jenni and jaimie create exquisite, complicated art.

We know how to calm our minds. The trick is to do the work. This is where weeding comes in. If ever there was a perfect metaphor for taming our minds, weeding is it. Creating an environment where weeds have to expend some effort to live is the beginning of weed control. This is sort of like keeping pornography out of our homes if we are too attached to sex, or cookies out of our freezers if we keep finding additional fat on our butts. Mulching is the solution we're looking for. A protective layer. Movies that entertain without sex. Gorp-based, small cookies. There's no need for anything fancy here. In gardening mulch is basically a hodgepodge of leaves and branches chopped into small pieces. It is terrific because it feeds dirt as it decomposes. Grass clippings are the ice cream of mulch. Even sawdust can work as long as you don't go nuts. Earthworms love mulch, and gardens love earthworms. Around here, people buy earthworms to give their gardens a boost in health and well-being.

Mulch can protect slopes from soil erosion and the soil from being compacted from foot traffic. It promotes water retention so we don't have to water as often. Best of all, mulch is great for keeping weed growth down to a dull roar. Experts tell us to mulch every spring. I mulch anytime, anyplace, making sure to keep it a few inches away from the trunks of trees and shrubs. In the same way, I work hard to keep anything but small gorp-based cookies away from my freezer. Alan allows only PG movies into his house. This kind of homework gives our brains a chance to quiet down.

≫

Even with mulch, as is true with our minds, consistently healthy gardens are the product of serious and constant weeding. Because in the Northwest everything grows like it is on growth hormones, serious gardeners have a list of weeds we go after, even if we spot them in public gardens on a Sunday stroll.

English ivy tops the list. Who would guess that such a beautiful, leafed vine, so perfect for hanging baskets, can strangle huge trees given half a chance? Ivy is an ecological nightmare waiting for its moment to pounce. I know this. A young couple in West Seattle asked us to clear out some of the ivy on their property. It had completely enveloped fences, walls, and trees. Beautiful and deadly. We carved the tree free first. It then took days to clear out most of the rest of the ivy. It had literally pulled down a fence in parts and pushed up the wooden flooring of a porch, making holes where needed so the ivy could keep growing upward. In a single day, one small yard's worth of ivy filled our pickup truck not once but twice. And we aren't finished. We'll probably never be finished, given how fast it grows.

Ivy plants can weigh in at 2,100 pounds. As it winds its way through our yards, driveways, parks, and ravines, ivy can cover the ground so completely that nothing else can grow. Except rats. We've found a couple of those. And mosquitoes. We've found those, as well. Not keeping ivy containered is like giving a fourteen-year-old car keys. Too much freedom.

In Seattle, second only to the curse of ivy is the curse of bind-weed. It is everywhere. Newcomers to the area often mistake it for morning glory since that is what it looks like. Except it isn't morning glory. It is its evil twin. Bindweed lurks in corners, and under ivy (!), waiting to pounce. Even when it is cut back, the weed has an ability to grow that would be inspiring if it came in the form of, say, dollar bills. Even tiny pieces of bindweed left on the ground will grow new plants. Ciscoe, the great gardening guru, warns people that if they ever see bindweed on their property, they can never go on vacation again. If they ignore his advice, he promises that they will never find their homes because they will be completely covered in the weed when they return. Strong words.

I love dandelions stir-fried or battered and fried, so I don't want to think of dandelions as weeds. These little plants are good for liver cleansing and are a natural diuretic. They are rich in vitamins and minerals, notably potassium and magnesium. My grandmother used to eat dandelion salads, and I lived with a woman who swore that dandelion tea is what kept her weight stable. Maybe, although I don't think I ever saw her eat a full meal. All I know is that, stir-fried, dandelion roots are, in a word, delicious. They remind me to take a second look at anything I've labeled "weed." There is probably another, "nonweed," use for it. Even mind-weeds can be turned around. If I can't meditate because I have the mind-weed of obsessing about how to pay for a new car, I can look at that weed more closely when I'm done meditating. Maybe it is showing me something I need to see. Maybe I don't really need a car. Or maybe I can share a car with one of my neighbors. That way we'll both decrease our costs of living

and probably become more efficient with our use of fuel. Even ivy
has a positive side. It can spunk up a container like nothing else or
turn a hanging basket into a miniature garden. Constrained, ivy is a
far cry from the noxious weed we pull once a month at the park
down the street.

Here's a dandelion recipe to try after a day of weeding:

Stir-Fried Dandelions

2–3 handfuls of cleaned dandelion roots, sliced like tiny carrot sticks

4 tablespoons sesame oil (Canola oil can also work. Olive oil is too
strong for me, but you might like it.)

1 teaspoon spunky pepper, like cayenne

5 cloves garlic, chopped

1 small onion, chopped into thin slices

¼ cup sesame seeds

First, cook or steam the roots until they are tender. This takes about
ten minutes. Drain and sauté in the sesame oil with the garlic and
onions and pepper. Add the sesame seeds at the end when everything is glistening and hot. I love the dandelions over long, thin buck-
wheat noodles. Rice also works. Couscous probably would, as well, but
I've never tried it. Season to taste.

Most people I know think of dandelions as a weed that needs
to go, recipes be damned. All I can say is, make sure you get the
taproot out of the ground or you'll need my stir-fry recipe. Ditto for
crabgrass and oxalis, if you think of them as weeds. I love these little
four-leaf-clover-like plants myself, but I may be alone here. There
are other weeds that need pulling. Pigweed, for example, can grow
to be ten feet tall. Shepherd's purse, which actually looks like the

bags carried by shepherds in very old paintings, will take over like the other weeds if you let it.

The county where I live literally gives away lists of weeds they want all of us to help eradicate. Water lilies and Eurasian water milfoil can foul up boat motors, snag fishhooks, impede canoe travel, and even tangle up your dog. I think of these weeds as the Earth-based equivalent of angry thinking. "Don't give noxious weeds a home," the county cries. These brats can kill fish by increasing water temperatures, throwing everything out of balance. "Get 'em!" is the cry of many a Saturday volunteer day at the water's edge.

Poison hemlock is on the list, as well. Revenge manifested as a weed. I've always thought it was Queen Anne's lace. It isn't. It just looks like it is. Poison hemlock will poison you if you eat it, so don't. Hemlock loves the sides of roads and empty lots—anyplace that has been ignored for a while, actually. So does hogweed, which at least has a nasty name to warn you that it might not be a good thing for a garden. Giant hogweed is evil; find a picture of it so you know what it looks like. Hogweed gets tall. Think fifteen feet, with lots of pointy leaves leading up to a flower that looks sort of like the top of a poison hemlock on hormones. I'm telling you, find a picture. Hogweed actually burns your skin bad enough to scar it. In the Northwest it is everywhere. So are garlic mustard and policeman's helmet, more weeds to look up.

Driving across the country a while back, I saw purple loosestrife everywhere. It always reminded me of romantic obsessive thinking, the way it could pop up unexpectedly—and everywhere. It is lovely, with its bright yellow and purple flowers. You just want to cut it for a huge bouquet. The only problem is that, like obsessive thoughts, purple loosestrife is a bully. It takes over without apology. Think mean girl in plant form. It will pretend to be your friend while stabbing you in the back, pushing everything in its way into the ground and then stomping it. If you think I'm joking, grab an iced tea and go watch some purple loosestrife for an afternoon. The cruelty you see will make you weep. Or at least give up any fantasies of further bouquets.

Lastly, common blackberry bushes are a gift that, untamed, have morphed into a curse. As someone who loves blackberries, I couldn't believe I'd ever think of the bushes as weeds.

I was wrong, so wrong.

Too much of a good thing is too much. Given half a chance, a small blackberry on your patio can grow so fast it could strangle your cat by morning. I have now seen entire roadways covered with bushes that started with one "let's plant a blackberry bush for pies, dear" moment. One friend has lost half her yard to the bushes. She is seriously considering hiring a team of goats to eat everything down to the ground. Before she does, I'll ask her to give me one last blackberry-picking day so I can make my third favorite dessert in the whole world (after chocolate cake and pumpkin pie), skillet cobbler. After that, the bushes be damned, I say. Besides, I know they are likely to grow back as soon as the goats leave. She is too good a friend for me to mention this. Plus, I don't want to lose access to the berries. Blackberries are my proof that some weed thinking can be transformed to nurture us. Romantic obsession can morph into compassion. Anger can shift into wisdom. Boredom can lead us into the learning of a new craft. With some mind-weeds, a little transformation can lead us directly into a gourmet's life.

Skillet Blackberry Cobbler

Preheat your oven to 400 degrees

Ingredients:

2 tablespoons cornstarch

¼ cup cold water

1½ cup sweetener (I use brown sugar, but Splenda could probably work. So could maple syrup. Probably.)

A squirt of lemon juice

3–5 cups blackberries, cleaned

1 cup whole wheat flour

1 teaspoon baking powder

6 tablespoons canola oil

¼ cup boiling water

To start, stir the cold water and cornstarch together in a big bowl until the cornstarch is dissolved. Then gently add one cup of sweetener, the lemon juice, and the blackberries. Put the whole mess into a cast-iron skillet. Then, also in a bowl, mix the flour, remaining sweetener, baking powder, and oil together. Add the boiling water. You'll end up with something that looks suspiciously like dough.

Heat the berries on the top of the stove until they are bubbling. Drop spoonfuls of the dough onto the boiling berries, and then bake the whole concoction, in the skillet, in the oven for 20–25 minutes. Since I have yet to make a cobbler without making a mess on the oven floor, which then sets off the fire alarm, I put a cookie sheet under the skillet to keep droppings to a low roar.

When the dough has turned golden, it is done. If you eat it immediately it will burn the top of your mouth so badly it will hurt for about ten days. For me this has always been a price worth paying.

The thing about weeds is that they are everywhere. Untamed, they take over. As such, they are a perfect metaphor for the constant mind-weeds you and I try to cope with every day. Too many weeds lead to a life unlived. How can we not weed?

Our crew leader, Cindi, meets me at a house that is a half block away from one of the most beautiful views I have ever seen—a huge bay outlined by snow-covered mountains. Behind them, a pink-gray sky. It is early and it is cold. Cindi tells me that our job is to clean out a rock garden. At first glance, it looks like we can do it in a day. The garden is only about twenty feet long and three feet deep.

A closer look tells us that the estimate of a day is delusional. The garden is choked with crabgrass. We look at each other and get out the shovels. An hour into digging, I am drenched with sweat. It doesn't matter that it is December and I can see my breath. Crabgrass clings to the dirt like there is no tomorrow. If I don't dig down at least four inches, the garden won't have a chance. I laugh as I work, thinking about my own weedy mind. I spent the entire drive to the house worrying about an unkind thing I said to a neighbor. Over and over I corrected my words in my head. When I was finally able to telephone her to apologize, she told me she didn't remember me saying anything unkind. "I'm from New Jersey," she tells me. "We all have thick skins."

I thank her and cringe. I missed an hour of a breathtaking sunrise obsessing about hurt feelings that didn't exist. "Oh, those mind-weeds," I say to myself and dig deeper.

Cindi focuses on a patch of hen and chickens, mat-forming succulents that are perfect for rock gardens. The parent rosettes are the hens. The smaller rosettes that spring from them are chicks. When they aren't being choked to death by crabgrass, they can spread quickly and are an easy addition of color and interest to any patch of ground, with their red and green foliage and tiny rosette shapes.

Hen and chicks are an acquired taste. They grow on you the more you are around them, the more you notice their tiny, delicate details. I know only random facts about them—that they are indigenous to Europe, for example, and that they were traditionally planted on thatched roofs to protect homes from lightning-induced fires. I know the protection was real. Hen and chicks are also deer resistant. They are easy to transplant. You can pluck a chick and set it down on any spot of well-drained soil. Unless the sun is completely blocked, it will grow.

Cindi is quiet, carefully pulling weeds and grass out from under and around the succulents. I am, for a while, frenzied with shoveling, trying to get rid of the grass. By 2:00 p.m., though, I admit to myself that my hyperactive approach isn't working. I'm leaving behind random clusters of grass that I'll have to go back to hand-pull. Plus, I've made a huge mess. Dirt is everywhere.

In comparison, Cindi's patch is perfectly cleaned of weeds and grass. It looks beautiful because she has also been mindfully shaping it along the way. I laugh. If I'm going to get rid of the weeds, I need to pay attention to one small patch of dirt at a time. In the same way, if I'm going to get rid of my junk-mail thinking, I can only do it one thought at a time. As this is dawning on me, Cindi looks up. It is almost four. We'll come back and finish this, she tells me. It will take a second day. She doesn't scold, complain, or frown. She just pulls the weeds one at a time, giving me permission to do the same thing. Already I'm calmer.

One workday later, we are finished. The yard looks beautiful. We go for coffee. Lattes. A small reward for hard training practice.

If you have a garden, you'll get weeds. No big deal. Just pull them out. If you have a mind, you'll get junky thinking. No big deal. The way to weed such thinking is to simply notice when we've gone off on a tangent. Simply recognizing mind-weeds is equivalent to weeding. Seeing the thoughts and knowing how unhelpful they are, we let them go. We stop feeding them the fertilizer of attention. As a result, our minds calm down, and as they do, we watch our lives become lighter, happier, and, surprisingly, more interesting. A growing calmness, combined with seeing clearly, allows us to know what we need to be doing moment by moment. It is pretty amazing, the way this plays out. We find we don't need to overplan our lives beyond an outlined sense of direction. We know where we want to go, what we want to do. So our work becomes paying close attention to what goes on around us to see the doors that open to help us head where we are meant to head. The doors we want to walk through.

Ditto for gardens. The plants we love have a chance to grow without being strangled by bullies like ivy, crabgrass, and bindweed. When the weeds are gone, you'll be amazed at how quickly everything else takes over. Beauty is there, expanding by the minute.

seven

Tomatoes Grow at Their Own Speed: Patience

If gardeners spent less time running about doing things they think they are supposed to do and more time contemplating the beauty of the world's plants, they'd get more out of their gardens and be less of a pest to the civilized world.

—Henry Mitchell, *One Man's Garden*

Shantideva spends a lot of time talking about patience in *The Way of the Bodhisattva*. He starts off by telling us that no matter what good we've done—even if we've been generous for thousands of years—it can all be destroyed in a moment of anger.

You and I knew this already. I would gladly walk over burning coals if it meant I could take back words I've said in anger. Even when I've been correct about a situation, the anger made it impossible to find a way through the negative to a more positive place. Ditto for the times when someone has aimed their anger at me. I've left stores, jobs, states, and a marriage as a result of someone's angry outbursts. Couldn't take it. Nope.

Anger destroys peace. It feeds negative fantasies and hatred. It can prevent us from sleeping, eating, hearing, noticing. We don't take care of ourselves when we are angry. We may not take care of our children. We abandon friends, pets, and gardens when we are filled with anger. We don't like ourselves. We may not like anyone.

The antidote is patience.

When I started to see the damage done by my anger, I vowed to stop getting angry. It wasn't anything fancy. I just sat myself down and said, "Enough." After that, every time I could feel anger starting to inch its way up my spine, I'd just think, "Enough." As simple and obvious as my solution has been, it has worked. Routing anger this way hasn't meant giving up compassion or an urgency to be of service to the world. It's just that I live my life assuming the positive and doing my best to see Buddha in everything and every being. When anger climbs up my spine anyway, I wait it out until it subsides, using its energy to do something physical like pull grass out of driveway cracks.

Patience. I suspect that Buddha knew, some twenty-five hundred years ago, that we would all be pretty impatient. As a result, he was forever giving us teaching aids. One is called the Six Paramitas, or perfections. They serve as catalysts for deepening our spiritual understanding of ourselves and the world around us. Included are:

- May I be generous and helpful.
- May I be pure and virtuous.
- May I be patient. May I be able to bear and forbear the wrongs of others.
- May I be strenuous, energetic, and persevering.
- May I practice meditation and attain concentration and oneness to serve all beings.
- May I gain wisdom and be able to give the benefit of my wisdom to others.

The secret catch of the paramitas is that they affect our lives the most when we give them time and space to work. There is a wonderful monk, So Sahn, whose life demonstrates the power of the paramitas. So Sahn lived in Korea in the 1500s. He is much loved by Koreans, mostly because he saved the country from being completely overtaken by Japan in 1592. He also happens to be a deeply wise and compassionate teacher, someone who says it like it is. So Sahn lost both of his parents by the time he was ten. Because he was smart he was sent, at twelve, to a school for up-and-coming Confucian scholars. By the time he was eighteen he was studying Zen. At twenty-one he took the Buddhist precepts to become a monk.

By the time So Sahn was thirty, he was deeply enlightened and becoming a leader in the Korean Zen tradition. After three years, though, he quit, fed up with organizational politics, and went into the mountains to live the life of a simple monk. The paramitas provided principles for his day-to-day living. At sixty-nine, in response to a plea from just about everyone who knew him, from

the king down, he agreed to come back down the mountain to help
fight the Japanese, organizing thousands of monks into an army
capable of pushing the invaders back into the sea. Even in war,
however, So Sahn kept the paramitas:

> *The Japanese were overwhelmed at the sight of these legions of*
> *Buddhist monks marching through the countryside, defending*
> *their country, yet committing no atrocities against their*
> *invaders. Those attackers who had the good fortune to fall into*
> *the hands of Master So Sahn's army were not beheaded or*
> *even tortured (as was the minimum custom afforded most*
> *prisoners of war in those days) but treated with humanity and*
> *compassion.* (The Mirror of Zen: The Classic Guide to
> Buddhist Practice by Zen Master So Sahn, *trans. Boep Joeng*
> *and Hyon Gak [Boston: Shambhala, 2006], xx)*

So Sahn left behind tight, powerful teachings. Just a few thousand words maybe. But they are words that have the capacity to
inspire us to have faith in our own hearts and in our spiritual work.
Many have to do with patience: "If you have no patience, the
limitless compassionate functioning of the Six Paramitas cannot be
attained." Patience lies at the bottom of everything. Everything.

Gardening is one of the few places where patience is visibly
rewarded. We may not start out as patient gardeners. I have a relative
who fussed so much about how slowly her tomato plants were
growing that her sons went to the market and bought a bunch of

tomatoes, which they proceeded to tie to the plants in an effort to help her relax. Last year I got a phone call from a new gardener who told me that she was tired of waiting for the flowers on her plants to morph into tomatoes. So she cut them all off to take them inside, where she put them under a grow lamp. She wanted to know how long it would take for the flowers to turn into tomatoes. More specifically, would they be ripe by the weekend? It was Wednesday.

It helps to be around people who are patient. Late one October my landscaping boss, Christie, asked if I would like to help decorate a huge Frank Lloyd Wright arts and crafts house snuggled up along the edge of Lake Washington. I was happy to say yes. We had two days to completely decorate some ten thousand square feet of house as well as replant the plants in the pots surrounding the house. Out with the nemesia, in with the pansies. Hello, mums. We worked hard. And fast. On my way out the door on day one, I reported back to Christie with a verbal list of everything we could check off our long list of tasks. I was feeling pretty smug because my list, anyway, was done.

Except I had totally forgotten about a line of pots just outside the family-room windows and had planted the pansies in the wrong place.

Christie was patience incarnate. After an initial cringe, she said she would clean up after me the next morning. I felt terrible and apologized profusely.

And felt terrible an hour later. Four hours later. That night. The next day. Christie was way past my mistakes. I was clinging to them.

I had forgotten that patience includes being patient with ourselves. We need to let go of our mistakes once we've cleaned up after ourselves as best we can. In gardening we dig up the pansies and replant them where they were meant to go in the first place. Then it is over. In other aspects of our lives we make our apologies, hopefully quickly and sincerely, think about how we can do better next time, and move on. If we can't be patient with ourselves, how can we expect to be patient with other people? The truth is, we can't. Life is too short to kick ourselves around the block for missed pansies or weeding plants that weren't weeds or overtrimmed hedges—the ones that are now two feet instead of the requested four. At least they are straight.

Mr. Kung is my personal patience saint. If Archie McPhee made a bobblehead version of him, I would buy dozens and line them up everywhere—along the backseat of my car, on the porch, along every window. Mr. Kung is a Chinese man in his mideighties who suffered through two years of trying to teach me Mandarin before we both threw our hands up in defeat. During those two years, now nearly twenty years ago, we became fast friends. I have never seen him get angry, not even when he was wrongfully evicted from subsidized housing because he didn't understand a piece of paper-work. I've never heard him raise his voice. I don't think I've ever seen him frown. As far as I can tell, the reason is because he figures that what needs to get done will eventually get done. He'll just stay with it for as long as it takes or until, like my Chinese learning, it becomes very clear that another path needs to be taken.

"As long as it takes" is the Secret Santa, if you will, of patience. It is the secret skill that can give us what we need to be patient. In the Catholic tradition it is quite common for people to identify particular saints as their personal protectors. I've always loved that idea. When I decided to drive across the country alone a couple of years ago, I thought hard about who might protect me on the drive. I had no planned route. I didn't know where I would be staying at night. My car was old. The clutch was going, and I had the Rockies to cross. I decided that I needed a really strong role model to inspire me, someone who had also taken off on his or her own to fearlessly cross mountains and rivers, as opposed to my neurotic tendency to make lists of everything that could go wrong.

Wonhyo was my man. I even made an appointment to get his name tattooed on my left ankle in case I totally freaked. I figured I'd calm down by looking down at my foot. Unfortunately, the tattoo artist never showed up. So I just trained myself to keep Wonhyo's name at the tip of my tongue whenever I was feeling a little scared. I only needed to remember him 4,232 times. Not too bad.

Like So Sahn the warrior monk, Wonhyo was a monk who lived in Korea, except that he lived in the ancient kingdom of Shilla thirteen hundred years ago. Wonhyo had a hard life. As a young man he found himself fighting in one of the many civil wars of his time. Many of his friends were killed in its battles. Villages were destroyed. Crops were lost. People starved.

Wonhyo was so overwhelmed by the heartbreak of it all that he decided to go into the mountains as an ascetic. He shaved his head, and off he went.

Wonhyo, like Mr. Kung, has taught me the true meaning of "as long as it takes." Even after twenty years of practice, Wonhyo wanted instruction. He decided that he would visit a teacher in China, so he packed up and started walking.

As the story goes, one night as he was crossing a desert, he found a small oasis where he could spend the night. (Brace yourself because the story gets slightly gross here.) He found a tree and slept under it, waking up in the middle of the night, dying of thirst. Since the moon wasn't out, he couldn't see. So he crawled around, hoping to find some water, convinced some was nearby. He was sleeping on grass under a tree, after all.

Finally he found something. It was a cup with water in it. Delicious.

The next morning when Wonhyo woke up he saw that the cup was really a skull. And it wasn't water. I'll stop here.

He was so sick he couldn't think. In that moment Wonhyo realized that we literally create the happiness or sadness in our lives through our own thinking. No need for a master now. He headed home.

At this point most of us would probably figure that we've hit the end of our spiritual maturation story. We would be wrong.

Wonhyo, by contrast, was pretty wise. When he made it back to Korea, he became his king's most trusted adviser and the spiritual guide for the kingdom of Shilla's upper crust. His power grew, and wealth made his life comfortable. Hand-embroidered exquisite robes. The best food available. More assistants than he could ever use. Regular conversations with educated people. A king for a pal. Wonhyo still took the time to give public lectures. Whenever he did, the place would be packed. The brightest acolytes sought him out. Life was good.

Still not the end of the story.

There was a little old monk in Shilla who would walk through the villages barefoot in wrinkled rags, ringing a bell and chanting, "Great peace, great peace. Don't think! Great peace. Just like this! Great peace." Wonhyo decided to pay the fellow a visit. When he finally found him, the little old man was sitting beside a dead fawn, crying his eyes out. He told Wonhyo that he had found the baby deer looking for his mother, who had been killed by some hunters. The monk had decided to go down to the village to beg for some milk so he could keep the fawn alive. Because he knew none of the poor villagers would give him milk for an animal, he said it was for his son, which was just as bad. A monk with a son?

Every once in a while a villager would give him some milk. He managed to keep the deer alive for about a month, but it had become harder and harder to get offerings. In his last trek down to the village it had taken three days to get anything. When he returned to his little hut the deer was dead.

Listening to his story, Wonhyo realized that he was in the presence of a great teacher, someone filled with wisdom and compassion. He asked to be the monk's student.

Okay.

Instead of heading for a hermitage, however, the monk took Wonhyo straight to a brothel. When a beautiful woman answered the door, the monk turned to Wonhyo and said to him,

> "For twenty years you've kept company with kings and princes and monks. It's not good for a monk to live in heaven all the time. He must also visit hell and save the people there, who are wallowing in their desires." In other words we need to learn how to be compassionate, wise and patient without needing to run into the mountains. The real test is in the street. For Wonhyo this meant the real test was in a brothel. (Seung Sahn Dropping Ashes on the Buddha [New York: Grove Press, 1976], 62)

Wonhyo was stunned. He told the man that he had never done anything like visit a brothel before. The old man's response was simple: "Have a good trip."

Wonhyo needed to keep going, to be open to life, to keep deepening his understanding of the way life was for everyone so he could grow in wisdom and compassion.

Word on the street is that Wonhyo had the time of his life that night. It wasn't just the sex. He also drank alcohol and ate rich foods, realizing that both joy and sorrow are everywhere, not just in temples and high places. He became a patron saint for the rest of us that night, leaving in the morning to take up the old man's practice of singing and dancing through the villages, shouting, "Great peace." I'm so happy he kept going for as long as it took to get to that place of wisdom and compassion. I needed both when I got lost in Wyoming and had a flat tire in South Dakota.

Mr. Kung has the same capacity to be in the world with an "as long as it takes" way about him. It makes him patient with everything that comes his way. He didn't mind that it took him years to clear up the mishap with his housing. And he didn't mind that it took years, maybe ten, to sort out his immigration documents. He just waited the bureaucracy out, taking the next steps as soon as they became clear.

One year Mr. Kung asked me to help him develop a company to import cotton diapers from China. Because I loved the idea of reusable diapers (my brain had completely blocked how difficult it is to keep up with cloth diapers), I said yes. It took him over a year, I think, to locate a cotton-making factory in China that had the capacity to make the diapers and the connections to get them out of the country and into the United States. When he was pretty sure we were ready to start importing, he decided that maybe we should get some samples first. Months later, we received a package of diapers, each one so tiny that it would have barely fit Barbie's babies. We sent them back with measurements, and the next batch, another six months later, was made up of the biggest diapers I have ever seen. Folded over, they could have doubled as shawls. Mr. Kung wasn't even irritated. He simply tried again. This time the diaper size was correct but the cotton weave was so loose the diapers wouldn't hold anything. In round four we received cotton with a tight weave. The only problem was the tiny splinters randomly interspersed in the fabric. By the time we finally got samples that could work, someone else had beaten him to the market. Mr. Kung didn't mind. It took as long as it took to get the diapers. Okay. End of story. He moved on to industrial metal products, where he ultimately had better luck.

In an effort to keep getting on airplanes, I have made Mr. Kung's "for as long as it takes" my travel mantra. This means I no longer make assumptions about the time I'll arrive at my destination. I'll get there when I get there. What is amazing about this shift in my thinking is the gift it has been. The last time I had to spend hours on a tarmac waiting to take off, I was so unreactive that both of my seatmates asked me if I was okay. I'd like to tell you that they both nodded and smiled when I told them my mantra, but the truth is that they both moved slightly away from me and quickly immersed themselves in reading the catalog of gifts we could buy once we were airborne.

In *The Way of the Bodhisattva*, Shantideva won't let go in his teaching about patience. He scolds us for being impatient with other people, insists that we should never take unkind words personally, telling us that harsh speech and unpleasant words don't harm our bodies. We need to let them go, not for the sake of the person coming at us, but for our own sakes. We need to let our children grow up at their own pace, our mastery of musical instruments "take as long as it takes," and our lilacs spend the seven years they need to grow before they bloom.

Shantideva also makes the case that angry people will suffer in their dying. Given the number of heart attacks that are downing aggressive people, my guess is that he was really on to something. Besides, it is hard enough to die without getting caught up in negative emotions. They can make the difference between a good dying, where our passage out of this world is filled with grace, and an experience that is horrific for us and anyone around us.

Even if people destroy holy images, Shantideva instructs us to have no anger. If we are able to stay outside of the anger, it will be like a fire that doesn't spread to another house because everything that might cause the fire to spread has been removed. Shantideva has taught me to focus on my own reaction whenever I'm caught in an anger-filled situation. Even when I want to say to myself, "What a total jerk," I've learned to say, "God, I hate that person's anger," instead. This reaction has regularly protected me from getting caught in judging someone else. Working in retail has provided many opportunities to practice this particular form of patience. Halfway through my first week at the nursery, a landscaper came in looking for American red geraniums. The problem was that not only did we not have the variety he wanted, we didn't have any geraniums at all yet. His response? He threw a tantrum that would make any two-year-old proud. What kind of a nursery were we! Since I obviously didn't know my job, he wanted to talk to my supervisor. When she repeated that the geraniums weren't in yet, I honestly thought he would throw himself onto the concrete floor and start pounding.

All this for geraniums?

Standing there, listening and watching, I could feel my body tensing up as anger started to fly up my spine. But as I looked at him I could see how exhausted his eyes were, and his slumped shoulders told me that things weren't okay in his life. In the same moment my brain kicked in: "Enough." Instead of anger, I was suddenly filled with a sadness for him. His life must be pretty tough for him to shout at two complete strangers who were only doing their jobs. In that instant something inside him shifted, as well. He looked at both of us, said, "Sorry," and walked out. I never saw him again.

Patience. It took me three tries to get to the Woodinville Unitarian Universalist Church's Wednesday night meditation sittings. I had reasonable excuses. The first time I got lost about three-quarters of the way there. In the interest of practicing deep humility, I'll admit here that the place is only about twelve miles from where I live. At the same time, I had to drive around curvy unknown roads up a ridge and down its other side to get there—in pitch-black. Plus, street signs in

Washington tend to be small and are often hidden by tree branches that keep moving even when there isn't any wind (because of ghosts?). This is why it is still hard for me not to suck my thumb and wail whenever I have to find a new place.

The second time I didn't make it because of a five-day power outage that made me a little jumpy. I told myself they probably wouldn't be sitting anyway. I was wrong. Looking back, I see that both times it was my own impatience that did me in. If I had driven another five minutes on my first try, I would have seen the turnoff for the church. If I had taken the thirty seconds needed to call about the sitting on try two, I would have gotten a "come on down," but I didn't.

The third time, though, I vowed to find the place even if I ended up walking there. The vow worked.

The Reverend Alex Holt, the church's minister, is adorable. Slightly long-haired, a smile in his eyes, a grin on his lips. In addition to his full-on effort on behalf of the Unitarian Universalist family, he is also a student of Zen. His style is warm, funny, and simple. He is self-deprecating. I like him instantly. It doesn't hurt that his short meditation robe is purple and that he is wearing jeans and sneakers.

We wear our shoes into the church and sit on chairs. This is American Zen. It is comfortable. Because the room is a little cool I wrap my coat around my knees. Nine of us sit together for two sittings, with a little break between them. At the end, tea.

Then Alex calls us back into the hall. For the next while we are going to study the Metta Sutta, or Sutra on Loving-Kindness, he tells

ıe Metta Sutta, partly because it was the first Buddhist
teaching I was able to memorize.

The Metta Sutta

This is what should be done
By one who is skilled in goodness,
And who knows the path of peace:
Let them be able and upright,
Straightforward and gentle in speech.
Humble and not conceited,
Contented and easily satisfied.
Unburdened with duties and frugal in their ways.
Peaceful and calm and wise and skillful,
Not proud and demanding in nature.
Let them not do the slightest thing
That the wise would later reprove.
Wishing: in gladness and in safety,
May all beings be at ease.
Whatever living beings there may be;
Whether they are weak or strong, omitting none,
The great or the mighty, medium, short, or small,
The seen and the unseen,
Those living near and far away,
Those born and to-be-born,
May all beings be at ease!

Let none deceive another,

Or despise any being in any state.

Let none through anger or ill-will

Wish harm upon another.

Even as a mother protects with her life

Her child, her only child,

So with a boundless heart

Should one cherish all living beings:

Radiating kindness over the entire world

Spreading upwards to the skies,

And downwards to the depths;

Outwards and unbounded,

Freed from hatred and ill-will.

Whether standing or walking, seated or lying down,

Free from drowsiness,

One should sustain this recollection.

This is said to be the sublime abiding.

By not holding to fixed views,

The pure-hearted one, having clarity of vision,

Being freed from sense desires,

Is not born again into this world.

As the story goes, the Metta Sutta grew out of an experience in Buddha's lifetime. He was staying at the Jetavana Monastery, built for him by his good friend, rich guy Anathapindika. It was the rainy season.

Buddha told his disciples that it was okay to meditate wherever they were rather than try to make it back to home base.

But the forest was scary, especially to the young monks. They were afraid of the sounds, the storms, and the snakes. At one point they freaked and ran back to Buddha, looking for protection. His response was to give them the Metta Sutta, telling them that its power was so strong that they would be able to permeate the entire world with radiant love as they chanted it. Their love would be the love of kindness and sympathy and harmlessness. This is love in the form of affection and wishing happiness for others. It is the love of a parent for a child, the love we all share for kittens and puppies.

So they chanted. And felt safe.

In Woodinville, we chant the Metta Sutta together. After some quiet, Alex asks us what struck us in the sutta as we were chanting. One person mentions the line about being humble and not conceited. Another talks about how struck she was by the lines:

Even as a mother protects with her life
Her child, her only child,
So with a boundless heart
Should one cherish all living beings.

I am not surprised. I've studied the sutra for years, sometimes alone, usually with others. Each time those lines pop out, they are so strong.

Listening, I ask myself, "What did I notice?" At first, a smug response. "It is all terrific. Every line is its own teaching." I'm surprised to hear Alex say the same thing. He must read minds. The smugness disappears.

I make myself go deeper.

"Larkin, you have to choose. What line?"

What line?

"May all beings be at ease."

At first nothing but the line. Then an insight so strong, I'm dizzy.

This is why I'm impatient when I am: I'm not at ease. It is probably why most of us are impatient when we are.

We aren't at ease.

When I'm at ease, missed deadlines are little blips on my mental screen instead of an excuse to eat an entire chocolate cake with my hands. When I'm at ease, a plumber who is a day late is no big deal. It's not like I don't have other things to do. When I'm at ease, you could say just about anything to me, from extremely kind to red-level nasty, and I'm okay. When I'm not at ease, a nasty comment can trigger my memory about how to make dolls I can stick pins into. All I have to do is decide where the pins need to go.

May all beings be at ease.

Patience is the pearl in this oyster.

A second insight: It isn't easy to get to ease, or we'd all be there already. In Buddhism there are some interesting teachings on this. The one that has helped me the most is called "opening up our view." This means literally letting go of our fixed ideas. All of them. This includes the ones about who is our friend and who is not. Or who is good and who is not—for example, that Democrats tend to be good but Republicans aren't or that dark chocolate is good for us but *South Park* isn't. The reality, for me anyway, is that I don't know. Period. I've been surrounded by Republicans all my life, starting with my father, who were kind, generous, and ethical. Ditto for the chief executive officers of large corporations I have known, Enron notwithstanding. Sometimes dark chocolate makes me so sick I can't look at it for weeks while *South Park* has a way of painfully spotlighting some of my own opinions in a way that would make any Zen master happy. I've lived long enough to experience deep friendships that have deteriorated into lost relationships in spite of best intentions. A woman who made my life miserable in a past corporate job has since become one of my closest friends. I just never know.

Neither do you.

When we open up our view, expectation falls away. All we can do is our best and then let go. As I write, Barack Obama has the aura of a rock star. Every person I talk to hopes he will be the world leader we are hoping for. This wasn't always so. Barack himself tells of "press conferences where nobody came."

We never know. Patience sits smack inside this reality.

In the meantime, I often remind myself that most Asian traditions teach that everyone on the planet has been our mother. This makes it easy for me to feel protective and loving toward everyone I meet, even when I don't have time to say more than a quick hello. When I'm at ease, everyone I run into is a delight. I notice the person sitting across from me at Cupcake Royale. She is wearing a yellow woolen sweater over a matching yellow cotton turtleneck. Her lips are bright red, her glasses large, the frames made of milky white plastic. She is wearing jeans and clearly waiting for a friend. Her half smile gives her away. She is, maybe, seventy. And a delight. The man on the other side of her has just offered his table to her. He is leaving soon. Heavily tattooed, laptop in hand, leather jacket, a different brand of jeans, he is also a delight. They feel like family, and they don't even know me. I feel the same way about the two little kids sipping cocoa behind me, and my heart hurts for the man who needs two canes to slowly walk to the counter for his order. He is young. His eyes are filled with pain and embarrassment. I ache for him. The two women across from me have just decided that coffee won't do it on this cold winter morning. They need cupcakes. My sisters. I also have a cupcake. We are so lucky to be dry and warm, to be sharing smiles. We get to be at ease together for this moment, and it is delicious.

Being at ease is so important that I am now putting it at the top of every New Year's resolution list. I already knew how good ease is for me—no tight shoulders or stomach cramps, no letters of apology that need writing, no sense of humor lost. It took sitting in the dark with the Reverend Holt to realize how important its impact is on the world around me—as it catalyzes my life, turning me into the patient person my mother thinks I am.

eight

Weeding at the Root: Anger

Peter once asked him, "Sir, how often should I forgive my brother if he keeps wrongdoing me? Up to seven times?" And Jesus said to him, "Not just seven: seventy times seven."

—Stephen Mitchell, *The Gospel According to Jesus*

One of the greatest pleasures of working in a nursery, aside from being surrounded on all sides by plants and flowers, is the people watching. Nurseries bring out the best in people. Maybe it is the beauty and all the oxygen in the air. A day at the nursery is a day filled with smiles, enthusiasm, and excitement. At the same time, I see things that I wouldn't have believed possible if I hadn't seen them with my own eyes. One is the number of women ostensibly living in an upper-class community who are poor. Another is the number of women who clearly forgot to stop being mean girls when they got out of high school.

First, the poverty. It took me a while to see this as more than an isolated incident. In my first week as the petunia lady, I watched a tiny elderly woman spend an hour and a half deciding which geranium she wanted for her porch. My initial reaction to her meticulous decision technique was impatience. Our geraniums were first-class, and red is red. Except red is not just red. When I started helping her, we found at least five different shades of red flowers. Some were warm, almost orange. Others were a burgundy red. Some had a neon glow. Some should have been called purple. Plus, all geranium plants are not equal. She was counting the number of buds on the flowers she liked the best.

As we counted I noticed things about her you wouldn't catch in a glance. How old her shoes were. A rip on the side of her blouse. It was sewn up and patched. Faded permanent stains along the bottom of her pants. When I helped her find a second geranium the following week, she was wearing the same clothes. This time we were looking for a white geranium. We spent almost an hour together counting buds.

Once I started noticing, I saw that every week we were visited by women this poor. Some of them had children. Most of them didn't. The first clue about their poverty was how long they took to choose a small, single plant. Their choices were always the least expensive choices possible. And they only bought one or, at the most, two. On a rainy Saturday I worked with a woman who had filled a cart half full of white delphiniums. She told me they were for the lawn outside her apartment building. It had taken her two bus rides to get to the nursery. Two hours after I had helped her load up her cart, she was still in the building, looking at shrubs and the fruit trees along the back fence. When she walked out, though, she carried only one delphinium; the rest she left in her cart.

Maybe the poverty in this country can't begin to compare with the poverty that surrounds us, but it is still here, right in the middle of where we live. In 2003, for example, poverty rates grew for the third straight year, with women far more likely than men to be poor. For single mothers, it is over a third of us. For women over sixty-five, 1 in 10. Almost 60 percent of adults who are poor are extremely poor, with annual incomes less than half the poverty standard. And while organizations like Millennium Promise take on the mission of ending poverty in our generation, poverty breaks my heart when I see it. And I see it everywhere.

The other phenomenon that really threw me was the amount of "mean girlitis" I witnessed. If you've ever been in a situation where another woman deliberately got in your way so you couldn't achieve a positive goal, you've been in the bardo of mean girls. If she put you down, mean girl. If she neglected to apologize, mean girl. And then if she refused to talk about any and all of this, very mean girl. For the record, mean girls aren't just female.

Ten Clues That You Are in the Presence of a Mean Girl

1. She is overly defensive.
2. She loves to talk about other people.

3. She loves revenge. It is as good as great sex for her.

4. She may be religious, but she is not spiritual.

5. She always has to look good.

6. Actually, it's always all about her.

7. She frequently flatters you.

8. She never forgives. Anything. Or forgets.

9. She is jealous when good things happen to you.

10. You feel worse after you've been around her.

While mean girls have their own charisma, they aren't fun. Maybe you knew one—or several—growing up. I used to know them as bullies. What's hard about mean girls is that they seduce us with the fantasy that we can be part of an in-crowd that matters, at least superficially. That is why the bullying always comes as such a shock when it surfaces:

> It happens when you least expect it, the sudden painful sting
> that hurts deeply, because you thought you were in a safe
> place, with other women and immune from harm. A word, a
> gesture, or some other seemingly innocuous behavior can be all
> it takes to wound in a way that hurts more than any physical
> loss. (Cheryl Dellasega, Mean Girls Grown Up [Hoboken, NJ:
> J. Wiley & Sons, 2005], 7)

Suddenly you find yourself excluded from a crowd you previously belonged to. You find yourself being teased or insulted by members of that crowd. Mean girls create cliques so they can have a way to exclude others.

Mean girls have to be in charge. A few years ago I suddenly realized that a friend of mine was a mean girl. Since we were well into our forties, clearly no longer teenagers, it took me a while to understand the situation we were in. She was my queen bee friend. I already knew that much. And to tell you the truth, I appreciated it. I didn't have to make any decisions when I was spending time with her. We did what she wanted to do, when she wanted to do it. I was okay with that because we liked doing the same things. That's what made us friends in the first place.

One day, though, I called her on a conversation in which she had been just plain nasty to me in front of another woman. Here are my words: "Please talk to me privately and seriously if you think I have a problem." Her response was to shrug it off, saying that she never intended to be hurtful. But two days later, when we were driving back to her house from a movie, without warning she drove us to a coffee shop, where she informed me in no uncertain terms that she was unsure how long it would take her to get over my words. If we had been in a play, neon lights spelling "mean girl" would have started flashing over our heads. She had no interest in my reaction. Then and there I knew our friendship was over.

Since that incident I've grown mean-girl antennae. I've seen the behavior in offices, at gas stations, on the path at Green Lake where I walk Bodhi every Tuesday. Women have told me stories that make

my breath stop. A neighbor told me about an office manager who
told lies about her to the company owner—just because. It wasn't
like they were competing for jobs; my neighbor is simply an attrac-
tive, competent accountant, and the manager just didn't like her. She
gossiped about her and teased her in hurtful ways, all the while
pretending to be joking. Eventually she "teased" her right out of the
job. It just wasn't worth staying. The company lost a terrific staff
person. When I lived at the Still Point Zen Buddhist Temple in
Detroit, one of the seminary students quit her job because of the
same behaviors. Co-workers bullied her right out of a job.

Mean girls are everywhere.

One sunny Saturday three women arrived at the nursery to buy
several huge pottery planters. At first I thought they were sisters.
They were young, thin, blond, all wearing the same black sweatpants
with the same white stripes.

Picking out planters isn't easy. You have to think about the colors of
the building they will sit near, the types and colors of plants that will be
planted in them, and the type and color of the ground around them.
Subtle color and texture changes can make the difference between lovely
and breathtaking. The three friends spent about forty-five minutes
looking at planters. Then the queen bee picked out two square, gray,
concrete planters. Each one cost close to two hundred dollars. She asked
the two other women what they thought. Sidekick responded that they
were perfect. The third woman, though, reminded her that she had
purchased two almost identical planters at a different store a few weeks

ago, only to return them later. Instead of a thank-you for the reminder, she got a loud, "Why did we bring you, again?"

On another morning I'm moving huge trees to a ramp in the front of the store. Palms, mostly. We are getting ready for a massive sale of indoor plants. The space looks great, crammed full of leafy, smiling trees waiting for new homes. Three women are standing near the palms. I try not to listen to their conversation, but I'm a born eavesdropper. If I don't make it to heaven when I die, this will be why. I can't help myself. I must have an eavesdropper gene. Anyway, one of the women is clearly upset. To be fair, part of me is listening to see if I can be helpful. I can't. She's angry at a friend who is in the restroom. The group was supposed to be eating at the Mexican restaurant across the street. Instead, they are suddenly in this line! Why wasn't she asked for her opinion? She looks at the other woman.

"Did she ask you about coming here?"

A nod of no.

My antennae start to quiver. A mean-girl sighting. I want to stay to see how this melodrama plays out. A half of a truck's worth of trees are waiting for me in the back. I need to leave.

I'm angry, though. Meanness really sets me off. First, all the poverty. Now, all the bullying.

What to do?

When I was in the seminary one of my biggest surprises was how often my teacher got angry. At first I thought it was just him, but then I met other Zen masters, some from the East and some

from the West. They got angry, too. I went back to the stories of
Shakyamuni Buddha's life. He got angry, too. He even called his
cousin Devadatta names: "You lickspittle!" Devadatta had tried to
kill him three times by then. Someone blatantly trying to kill you
can do that to Buddhas.

They get angry.

So the point for you and me is not that we shouldn't get angry.
We do. We will. There will be times when whispering, "Enough," to
ourselves won't work. And we may be angry for good reasons.
Darfur is not okay. Genocide is not okay. Guantánamo is not okay.
Poverty, unchosen, is not okay. Mean-girl behavior? Not okay.

The question is: What do we do with the anger?

Teachers from Shantideva to the Dalai Lama have taught me a
four-part process to transform anger into something positive. Small
steps leading to a significant shift. They offer an immediate, and
surprisingly positive, way to respond to situations in which I used to
fantasize about designing huge billboards listing all the harm done
to me, which I would drive through the city of the person who had
hurt me and park it in front of her house.

1. Admit it.

The first thing I do is admit I'm angry. This can be extremely
difficult for those of us who were raised to believe that nice people
don't get angry. I'm nice. I get angry. You are nice. You get angry. It is
okay. Even the Dalai Lama admits to getting angry sometimes. So we

are in good company. I suspect that admitting that we are angry instead of letting it fester unlabeled helps our health in all sorts of ways. Our emotional eating (i.e., putting food into our mouths instead of dealing with the situation in front of us) may lessen, and our hearts may be better protected from breaking down since, in the end, anger is really a form of heartbreak. When we admit it, we can heal. If we never do, we can't.

2. Put time and space between our anger and what caused it.

Once we admit we are angry, we need to put some time and space between our anger and the person or situation that caused it. My friend Haju Linda Murray once told me that it is impossible to feel anxious after ten deep breaths. I've found that these same ten deep breaths can give me the time I need to think more clearly about a situation so I don't swing back. It gives my system time to flush some of the energy of the anger, at least enough to breathe normally again. It keeps my mouth, the one that still has a penchant for swearing like there is no tomorrow, busy so I don't yell things I know I will regret.

3. Don't harm back.

Even though I know this is much harder than it looks on paper, our next job is to do whatever it takes not to harm back. An eye for an eye has never worked. Just saying the words "Don't harm back" is enough for me to take a giant step away from what is going on while I wait for my energy to transform into something more positive. This does not mean that I refrain from helping people who need to be in jail to get there. While this system's jails are my least favorite places in the country, followed closely by unkempt public housing developments, sometimes people have to be protected from harming others. Right now the only way I know how to help them is to facilitate their finding their way to a prison cell. When I lived in Detroit there was a man who openly pushed and shoved his wife and broke more laws than anyone I'd ever met, beginning with writing false checks. And then he started to sexually abuse his daughter. Because he was the patriarch of a large family and a charismatic community leader, we all gave him the benefit of the doubt—until his little girl entered the picture. At that point even good friends of the family stepped forward to help him find his way to a prison cell, where he couldn't harm anymore.

While I don't have enough money to pull another person out of poverty, I can patiently and lovingly help her to pick out the perfect geranium. When we're done I can give her a small white polished stone I just happen to have in my pocket. "It is a wish-fulfilling jewel," I tell her. "To make your dreams come true." And even though it might not make all her dreams come true, it tells her that someone out there, namely me, or namely you, cares about her and wants her to be happy. No amount of money can buy that.

I can't take the words of the mean girl back, but I can casually mention how lucky she is to have friends who care enough about her to give her honest feedback. I can say I miss the friends I have who do that for me.

When I go home, I can pray. "Please, let peace begin with me. I know I whine about this, but I mean it."

I've always had a thing about peace. When I was six years old my favorite song in the whole world started with the line, "Let there be peace on earth, and let it begin with me." I sang that song every morning, noon, and night at least for a year. That my mother didn't lock me in my room for the entire time is a testament to her otherworldly patience. As someone who has been chanting Buddhist chants for the last twenty years, I can't remember the rest of the song today. Even so, that phrase has a way of resurfacing, especially in holiday seasons, rain, snow, or shine.

4. Let peace begin with you.

The final step of the path out of anger is to practice peace. As I think about this, I realize that I've always taken the message literally, considering it a personal mantra of sorts. Over the years I've worked with peace groups, taken negotiation classes with Harvard professors (I'm not above bragging), learned how to mediate conflicts. The mediation and negotiation skills were hugely helpful through the nineties, first when I was management consulting and then when I moved into Detroit to start Still Point Zen Buddhist Temple in 1999. I was able to negotiate a deal with a drug dealer in the building next to us to stop doing deals on the days we held retreats. His traffic was distracting to our walking meditation. But even after all these accomplishments, the true measure of my peacekeeping, as opposed to anger-creating, skills,

however, is whether or not I can make it through the holidays with
family and friends intact.

Holidays can be tough. More than any other time of the year,
during holidays we don't want to get angry at anyone. We don't want
to argue.

But we do.

In my family, things aren't perfect early on. For example, some of
us eat meat. Some of us don't. Some of us have tried to fake out meat
eaters with Tofurky, only to fail publicly and soundly. We have
different tastes in clothes, music, movies, and books. I'm pretty sure
that the only thing we all have in common is that we love Jon Stewart.
I don't even want to begin to think about what that means.

In Buddhism, "Let peace begin with me" is about wisdom and
compassion. The basic teaching of Buddhism is to do no harm.
Period. We do this by bringing all the wisdom and compassion we
can muster into our daily lives. Doing no harm means being fully
present for each other in every situation, large and small. By being
present, we learn when to say or do something. We figure out how to
help the tiny woman looking for her perfect geranium. We tell
ourselves it is time to walk away from a mean girl before she does
any more damage. We get better at recognizing the times when we
need to keep our mouths shut. Last Christmas, "Let peace begin with
me" meant learning to say, "I hear you," to my daughter when we
disagreed about a topic. For her, homeopathic remedies are no more
than sugar pills. For me, they stop leg cramps. When I didn't reply to

her after she registered her opinion about my remedies, she was hurt by my silence. I realized that being quiet wasn't enough to dissipate the tension. I had to acknowledge her words. As soon as I started telling her I heard her, even as we disagreed, peace reigned.

Doing no harm is about making immediate apologies. In the seminary we were taught to apologize quickly for every single mistake we made—as well as for things we did that might turn out to be mistakes. The lesson wasn't about making mistakes. My teacher knew we would make plenty, and that was okay. The lesson was about creating a habit of apologizing quickly and sincerely. Every day I am grateful for this ability. Especially during holidays when I forget to preheat the oven for the three pies I've promised for dessert, which immediately means we'll only be having ice cream. The sincerity of my words nips all kinds of irritation in the bud, both mine and my guests. And it doesn't hurt that everyone gets to take pie home for the next day. This Christmas, "Let peace begin with me" meant sharing meals with people I didn't know and trying foods I wasn't sure I would like. I made new friends and discovered new treats. Cinnamon ice cream. Pumpkin pudding. It meant buying bags of groceries at the supermarket and then donating them to the food bank. I know from my own experience that it is pretty hard to be peaceful when you are hungry.

Wisdom and compassion are made of small moments like these. They become antidotes to anger. Saying, "I hear you." Trying the eggplant curry with a smile. Dropping a friend off at a car dealer before dawn on a cold rainy morning. Walking a neighbor's dog in the same rain. Secretly leaving a jar of bubble bath outside the door of a woman you heard weeping late the night before. In the middle of these small doings there is great peace because this is the place where heart meets heart. This is a place where anger has no place to land.

I can't mean-mouth my friend back, but I can go home and use my energy to scrub every window until it shines, and when I'm done I can write her a letter saying how sorry I am for any harm I've ever caused her. I can tell her that I will miss her because that is also true. With a clean heart, I can make new friends. So I do.

I'll admit it here. Every once in a while dealing with a mean girl calls for heavy ammunition, say, a saint who can take us by the hand and lead us back into the land of peace. Someone who has dealt with mean girls, mean boys, mean governments, a mean world and still embodies great peace and compassion. Sometimes we need to fall to the ground and call out her name:

Amma.

Most people know Amma as the hugging saint. If you ever find yourself in the same room with her, you'll experience for yourself that she is imbued with divine presence. She is divine presence. Amma doesn't try to convert anyone to her tradition, Hinduism. She only serves. Her charitable activities are up there with Gates and Oprah, even though she has never asked for donations, to my knowledge. She teaches her thousands of followers to "only serve," and they do. To date that has meant building over twenty-five thousand homes for poor families in India, creating pension funds for more than fifty thousand elderly women, building a hospital and colleges of engineering, working to create miles of land where only water existed before, bucket by bucket of sand.

I first heard about Amma when I was living in downtown Detroit. Her story: she was born in a poor fishing village on the south coast of India in 1953. She was thrown out of her house as a young girl for giving food and clothing to people who were more destitute than her family. She was ostracized and physically abused. Her father was the worst, followed closely by her older brother, who was so bad tempered that he even tried to stab her to death.

Amma used nature as her protector. She lived on, and loved, the land. And she loved all those mean people anyway. Gradually, followers discovered her. Now maybe a million people think of her as their guru.

When she came to Michigan on one of her world tours, the young people living at the abbey were adamant that we needed to see her and be hugged. They told me that she has been known to hug twelve thousand people at a time without taking any breaks. They told me that if you show up at one of her *darshans*, you are guaranteed a hug even if she has to stay in her seat for a day to get to you.

We decided to see Amma on a Thursday night in the middle of winter. She was going to be only about fifteen miles away from us. When we reached the hotel where she was holding *darshan*, we saw notices that said the service would start early, maybe 6:00 p.m. We aimed for that time. When we got there, thousands of people were already milling around the hotel, a Comfort Inn type of place, just off a highway. Each of us was given a number. Mine was in the two thousands. "Come back later," we were told. "She'll probably get to you somewhere around 4:00 a.m."

We stayed anyway, cramming ourselves into the corner of an already overflowing ballroom. We chanted away with the crowd, in love with the sounds and rhythms we had never heard before. Every half hour or so someone would walk through the crowd asking for volunteers for everything from serving coffee to giving out tickets to people who wanted hugs.

I signed up and was sent to a huge table where massive colanders of coffee and tea were keeping people awake until their turn with Amma. By then it was 12:30 a.m., and the hugging saint was in her groove. Because I am an early-to-bed, early-to-rise person, 12:30 a.m. is so far past my bedtime that I was giddy. Even so, I did my best. At first this meant only spilling a little coffee as I served it. Then it meant almost knocking over a carafe of tea. Then it meant not noticing that one of the cauldrons had sprung a leak until the table next to mine, the one with muffins and rolls, was flooded. At that point a kind young man walked up to me and took off my apron, officially firing me as an Amma volunteer. They were safer without my help. He thanked me for my effort anyway, gave me a hug, and aimed me back into the crowd.

Amma just kept hugging.

She hugged thousands of people, letting babies and people who were sick or disabled cut into line whenever they approached her from the side. People were carried to her. People crawled to her. She just kept hugging.

By 2:30 a.m. I was clear-eyed again since we were closing in on my natural wake-up hour, 4:00 a.m. I watched the crowd move forward slowly, a snake finding its way.

By 4:30 a.m. it was our turn. We were instructed to kneel in front of Amma. She looked at each one of us, and then as we were individually pushed into her arms by a disciple, she whispered into our ears. "My son, my son." Or ,"My daughter, my daughter," or maybe a mantra, a phrase we were to keep repeating. In that moment, emptiness. In that moment, divinity. It was impossible to fight it. When it was my turn she grabbed my hands and kissed them, moving me beyond words. She understood my heart, my yearning for a world of peace, my aching for happiness for every single person who calls the Earth home.

In a flash she was hugging the next person. And the next. And the next. When we left, shortly before dawn, Amma was still hugging, the way she does, the way she will until her last breath.

When you are with Amma there is simply no room for meanness in your heart. There is nothing but a sensation of abiding love and great compassion that is almost palpable. Even today, years later, whenever I feel myself starting to get snagged by negative emotions, if chanting doesn't clean me out, I picture Amma. Then, every time, I grin at myself, getting a kick out of how silly I am to use any energy

at all responding to whomever it was that tried to harm me. As
Amma says,

> *They are throwing their own mud, their own dust. It is their*
> *own mental stuff. It doesn't matter who says what. If mother*
> *listens to what others say (that is negative) then she will not be*
> *able to do her work. Mother's mission is to love and serve.*
> *(Amma, quoted by Judith Cornell,* Amma: Healing the Heart
> of the World *[New York: William Morrow, 2001], 200)*

A better role model doesn't exist.

nine

The Great Harvest: Joy

The seed of God is in us. If you are an intelligent and hard-working farmer, it will thrive and grow up into God, whose seed it is, and its fruits will be God fruits. Pear seeds grow into pear trees, nut seeds grow into nut trees, and God seeds grow into God.

—Meister Eckhart, *The Gospel According to Jesus*

Raindrops on roses and whiskers on kittens. Bright copper kettles. Warm woolen mittens. I am sitting in an old oak chair, looking out three six-foot-square bay windows. Outside, an ice storm. Everything sparkles. It is glorious. At 2:00 a.m. there are no cars on the road distracting me with concern about the passengers. It looks like Santa Claus did a diamond run and then dropped them all over the park across the street. The street lamp provides just the right amount of light to bounce back and forth off the branches and the walkways.

I am so filled with joy I can't sleep. So I watch until, finally, at 5:00 a.m. I rest for an hour. For those three hours, though, whiskers on kittens and warm woolen mittens writ large had filled me with so much love and compassion for I don't know what, that it was all I could do to sit still. What I wanted to do was make a gazillion snow angels but decided not to, at the last moment, because the pristine scene was so perfect.

Every day there is joy. It always surfaces as a surprise. I haven't figured out how to will it. What I do know is that it arises out of everyday moments and everyday things. After a rain, the smell. Watching my puppy trying to get to a bone that has lodged itself under the couch. Yesterday this feeling popped up when I was decorating someone's house for the holidays. She lives in a beautiful Victorian house overlooking Lake Washington. Floor-to-ceiling windows merge indoors and outdoors. Her tastes are natural colors. As a result, furniture, curtains, and floors don't distract from the natural beauty outside.

Except at Christmas. When the holidays arrive, everything shifts. Candles and smells and gold and silver sparkly things are pulled out of closets, and away we go. My job is to cover a sixteen-foot ledge dividing the kitchen from the family room with garlands and toys. I put teddy bears in small sleighs and line up toy Santas like a miniature marching band, with the electric ones in front so they can be plugged in by even the smallest child. If you haven't seen a toy Santa hula dancing to "Jingle House Rock," you haven't lived. Evergreen garlands provide a ground cover for the toys. A huge bowl filled with gold and red sparkle-filled ornaments in two sizes becomes the centerpiece. Putting the bowl on the ledge, I am filled with happiness and a gratitude that comes from being a part of the team creating a beautiful environment for a wonderful family.

As I make up holiday-themed nosegays to fill three cardboard horns woven into the garlands, it hits me hard. Joy. Tiny red euca-lyptus leaves. Joy. Miniature gold balls to be tucked into the nose-gays. Joy. Joy. Joy. Joy. And it isn't even my house.

We don't have to run after joy. It just shows up when we put down our negative emotions and concentrate on what is right in front of us. It is 6:00 a.m. I am sitting in my pink Valentine's Day bathrobe at the dining-room table in the dark. It is pouring out, and the dog has to pee. I didn't sleep much last night. Yesterday every-body in the building was informed that each of us needs to come up with at least five thousand dollars for a new roof. It is leaking and has rotted in spots. We have a month to come up with the cash. The emergency assessment is nonnegotiable.

After I return home from the meeting where we were told about the emergency assessment, three single friends call. Each one is unhappy. They know they shouldn't feel bad about being alone on Valentine's Day, but they do anyway. Two say, "Where are all the good men?" One says, "Where are all the good women?" They sound like they have been crying, or maybe they just have colds.

Sitting in the dark, alone on Valentine's Day morning, I realize that my life has become its own country-and-western song. My dog has to pee. I don't have a roof. My car is a wreck. My mother needs surgery. I've just been fired. (Okay, I haven't been fired. The truth is that it is impossible to weed when the ground is frozen. The ground never freezes in Seattle—at least not until this year. This year it is frozen solid. Boo hoo hoo.)

The dog looks at me and throws up.

"Fine," I say. "I get to be grumpy."

At 6:30 a.m. the phone rings. It is a radio station in Texas. Two good old boys, Jim and Mike, make my heart sing. They are funny, riffing off each other. They tell their listeners that they don't have to be Buddhist to like what I write. I'm grateful, given that their listener base is big-C Christian. They ask me for ideas for small good deeds people can do to celebrate loving each other. I tell them about a friend who makes cookies—the sugar ones with the pink frosting and the sprinkles—which she then proceeds to hand out to perfect strangers. I tell them about an incident that happened yesterday. A little girl was trying to cross a complicated intersection—four lanes of traffic. I was walking the dog across the street kitty-corner from her. As I stopped to figure out how I could get to her, a young jogger stopped, leaned down to her, took her hand, walked her across the street, and then jogged away.

"People are good," I tell Jim and Mike. "I think it is innate." They agree.

After about twenty more minutes of chatting, Jim tells me they need to say good-bye. He says I sound genuinely happy. I am, I realize, dog vomit notwithstanding. I feel them smiling over the phone lines. As we hang up, I'm grinning. Joy has sneaked back into my country-and-western life.

We have to let joy in. A partner can't bring us joy if we keep a list of all of his or her failings tucked in the back of our brain, ever watchful for additions. A new house, even an *Extreme Makeover: Home Edition* version, won't bring us joy if we hold on to our bitterness about past heartbreaks. Traveling won't make us happy if we arrive at our destination with unhappy thoughts or feelings. I always think of a story about a man who went to Aruba from London, only to discover that he was just as unhappy on the island as he was at home. His great insight was that it didn't matter where he went, he was following himself everywhere. Good to remember when we are thinking about tapping out our Visa card for a cheer-up week in Mexico.

Joy is a cheap date. It doesn't have to cost much. My friend David has been collecting baseball cards for half of forever. Whenever he talks about them, his eyes light up. He sounds happier than at any other time. Happier than when he reports back on dates, books, and new jobs. For the first twenty years, anyway, this was not something that cost him much money. I visit my friend Cheryl, and her eyes light up when she talks about gardening. The more detailed the conversation, the more light in her eyes. For Kent, particular smells send him into happy land. Actually, joy has a way of creeping up behind many of us via smells. The job of certain plants is to remind us that the world, beneath all our melodrama, is a pretty happy place. Carnations. Heliotrope. Sweet peas. Lavender. Everywhere, lavender. Scented geraniums. Rosemary by a front door. Thyme by a back door or, better yet, next to a garbage can or compost pile. Roses placed somewhere near the window where we read or write. Butterfly bushes.

> *All the joy the world contains*
> *Has come through wishing happiness*
> *For others.*
> *All the misery the world contains*
> *Has come through wanting pleasure for oneself.*
> —Shantideva, Pema Chodron, *No Time to Lose*, p. 319

The products of our gardens, however small, bring joy. My neighbor brings me a small basket of tomatoes. She has too many. I'm thrilled. Four hours later I'm making made-from-scratch spaghetti sauce for a friend who showed up to announce the presence of a new boyfriend in her life. Sheila is a young, spunky seventy. Her new friend is sixty-two. They sound like a good match. A colleague at the nursery brings me bags of fruits and vegetables from her backyard. I can't believe she took the time to pick a quart of

blueberries for me. With three teenagers and an unemployed
husband, she has a full life.

A few days later a driver for one of our suppliers appears with
bouquets of flowers for each of us. This single act of kindness puts us
all in a tizzy. It feels a little like someone has asked all of us to go steady.

The gift of flowers is a gift of joy. Flat-out. When I was fifteen
years old I had a crush on a way-too-old nineteen-year-old senior
named Jeff Panza. Although he would occasionally say hello to
me when I saw him, I was pretty sure he didn't know who I was.
Unknown freshman. Most popular senior. Then a dozen roses
showed up at my house on Valentine's Day. Oh, yes, the Earth stood
still. A declaration of intention and attraction. I didn't sleep for four
days. My parents responded strongly and unhappily. They wanted
his name, his number, his address, and times when his mother
would be home. They wanted an interview. He passed. Even though
our love story didn't last long, given my completely immature ways,
I kept those flowers for years.

Flowers. On February 12, 2004, the newly elected mayor of San
Francisco announced that his staff would be performing marriage
ceremonies for gay and lesbian couples, starting immediately.
Because it was commonly known that the courts would quickly
move to stop the process, couples rushed to city hall without having
time to plan.

To demonstrate support for them, donations of bouquets flew
in from all over the country. Most simply said, "To any loving

couple." Of the 4,036 partnerships legally acknowledged, half received bouquets. The thing is, the flowers weren't from the San Francisco gay community or even other gay communities. They were from college kids in Texas, eighty-seven-year-old grandmothers, and teens in Nebraska. They were from parents, kids, straights, and gays. They were from strangers who simply wished them well. No couple stayed dry-eyed receiving the surprise bouquets. Not one.

Helping others invariably feeds joy. A few evenings ago I walked past a young man crouched under an awning on Seattle's Broadway. He was sitting on a backpack. It was windshield-wipers-on-high pouring. He wasn't begging. Three steps past him, I cleaned out my change purse. I had a little over two dollars. I went back to him and said, "Please go get a cup of tea. We'll both feel warmer." He looked up and grinned. "Mighty nice." I walked away happy. Such a small doing.

At the nursery, every once in a while we cross wires with a supplier. Sometimes this means running out of bestsellers. Sometimes it means that we keep getting plants that we have stopped ordering. Last summer one of those plants was wandering Jews. Wandering Jews are terrific container plants. They grow fast, and their leaves have a lovely way of catching the sunlight. However, even after folks' containers and hanging baskets were planted for the season, the plants kept coming. It was like being caught in a Charlie Chaplin movie. I'm talking about thousands and thousands of wandering Jews. Racks full.

What to do?

Cheryl came up with the idea of giving them away to children. We'd give them a plastic four-inch pot, help them to cover it with stickers, then fill it with dirt and give them a plant for their bedrooms. We had the most fun possible with those kids. Each one was delighted with his or her new plant. Some didn't want to leave the planting table. They chattered away with us as we covered the pots with stickers, telling us about their lives, their schools, their teachers, their families. Most of them had intriguing names. When Cheryl asked one little girl about hers, she said it was a Maori word.

"Oh," said Cheryl. "Are you from New Zealand?"

"Oh, no. My mother went on a trip to New Zealand. When she came back, she had me."

We gave away almost all of the plants. It has been my favorite nursery day so far.

One of my biggest surprises, as I stumble along the Buddhist path, is the constant instruction to be joyful. It isn't a suggestion. It is an obligation. It took a while to give what was already happening more energy. Kick starts happened naturally when I looked toward other people, thinking, "How can I help?" The greatest surprise and—let me just say it here—relief has been that helping others does not have to be expensive. For example, every Christmas season I make a list of twelve anonymous good deeds I want to do as my own Secret Santa tradition. They range from buying a bag of groceries for a homeless family to dropping off Christmas cookies at the doorsteps of neighbors to taking cleaned-up Christmas ornaments I've been buying all year at thrift shops to a senior center. If I spend over a hundred dollars it's only because I just had to put a poinsettia in with the groceries. Each year I'm excited to get started. And each year, Secret Santa tasks accomplished, I feel like I've had the best holiday of my life.

So what prevents us from being more joyful? For most of us it seems to be worry. We worry about the Earth, our health, children, our cars, heat, cold, politics. We worry about our pets, violence, our yards, going broke, our boss, our co-workers, our neighbors. We worry about the little girl who was in the drugstore wearing sandals without socks on a cold winter day. We worry about her parents and her siblings, if she has any. We worry about our sons in prison. We worry about our parents, their health, their bills.

The list is endless.

Unfortunately, worry by itself doesn't change anything. Never has. Never will. And that is not the bad news. Okay, maybe it is. More bad news is that worry blocks joy.

If I'm worried about something, I could be surrounded by sparkles and sitting on Santa's lap while he is handing me the keys to a new Prius and I wouldn't feel joy. I probably wouldn't feel anything. Worry is that strong.

What is difficult about worry is that it is a sane response to many of the aspects of our lives. It can trigger more responsibility, and if it does, hurray. We start paying our bills on time, tell our daughter she needs to clean her room, tell our son that, at forty, he can get his own apartment. We can drive less, consolidate errand trips. We can give more away, adopt a charity.

But after that? We need to drop the worrying so joy can get through to us sooner rather than later. Refilling our mind with positive thinking helps. The Six Paramitas are one example of thoughts that break through worry. As a quick reminder, they include generosity, virtuous behavior, patience, energetic effort, meditation or prayer, and putting concentration into whatever we are doing.

For me, the first paramita, generosity, has always had the power to break through worry. I think it is because a lot of worry comes from feeling out of control. But I can control generosity. I can decide how much food I'll share, how many books I'll give away. Generosity, by its very nature, is focused on something other than ourselves. What a relief that can be! In fact, a picture of Tara sits on my desk to remind me to be generous every day.

Tara is one of the best-known Buddhist bodhisattvas. Although she takes innumerable forms, her most recognized one (the one seen most often on greeting cards, anyway) is Green Tara. Basically, she is a beautiful, naked woman, sitting on an open lotus flower, who happens to be green. As the story goes, Tara is the wife of another big-time bodhisattva, Avalokitesvara, and was born from a compassionate tear he shed just before he experienced full enlightenment. Tara is all about generosity—in any form.

She shows up pretty regularly in my life. A couple of years ago I got really sick going into winter—pneumonia and asthma at the same time. It was all I could do to curl up in a fetal position on my couch waiting for my body to start fighting back. My nurse-practitioner told me I should head for a hospital. Since I didn't have health insurance and wasn't quite "working poor" enough to get subsidized help, that wasn't going to work. I knew the hospital would cost thousands of dollars that I didn't have. I hate debt enough to gamble with my health.

We made a deal. I'd stay on my couch, drink half the fluids in Michigan, and ingest antibiotics strong enough to kill an elephant. If I didn't get half-better in four days, I would head for the nearest hospital, debt be damned.

Every day around noon, there would be a knock on my door. At first I wasn't going to answer it. Only two or three people knew I was sick, and they were forty-five miles away. But curiosity always wins, so I opened the door. Sitting on the porch was a cardboard box filled with vegetable soup, homemade bread, and a special treat, a cookie, say, or a tiny flower in a vase. Every day for a week, a care package showed up at lunchtime. One day there was also a huge box of chocolates at the back door. On another day UPS delivered two books of Gary Larson cartoons. To this day I'm not sure who left all the boxes. Tara, I guess.

Tara reminds me to respond generously to every situation I find myself in. This might take the form of packing an extra lunch on the days I landscape, just in case. Or it might mean finishing a writing job ahead of my deadline so my editor doesn't have to nag me to send the article in.

You know what *virtuous* means. Muddied minds, whether they are filled with drugs, alcohol, too much sugar, or pornography, create consequences that fertilize great worries. Enough said.

Mr. Kung's form of patience, "For as long as it takes," also helps me with worry. Zen stories are filled with this form of patience. At lunch with a friend, he tells me about a monk who built a hut in the Chiri Mountains in Korea, planning to develop it into a great monastery. Nobody (nobody!) showed up for the first thirty years! Now it is one of the country's great teaching centers.

Patience in the form of bearing and forbearing the wrongs of others can also take the energy out of worry. No matter what you and I do, people will have opinions. A lot of them will be negative. Okay. Once we realize that their opinions are a reflection of who they are and not who we are, worry goes away. This includes our children and their opinions about all the mistakes we made—and every parent has made plenty. Unfortunately, we can never completely please anyone else because everything changes and everyone changes, so even if, for once, we completely pleased someone last week, that was then and this is now, and whatever we did then probably won't do today. Not one of us will ever fulfill all the expectations of our parents, children, friends, colleagues, electorate. We can only do our best and move on. Let them talk, I say. It will give people like me stories to write about. Heh, heh.

Noticing and appreciating the goodness we see in others knocks the energy right out of worry. I am lucky to be surrounded by great generosity. Jaimie and Cindi, my landscaping comrades, constantly bring food to share for lunch, and if one of them drives off for a bathroom run, she invariably returns with coffee for the rest of us. When jaimie found out how much I love chocolate cake, she showed up with a gift certificate for a fresh cupcake from Café Royale, and it wasn't even my birthday. Cindi gives me plants and washes and dries all of our filthy, smelly gloves so we can have clean, dry ones the next workday, just because. The Dalai Lama advises us to "rejoice when we see others doing something good." I get to rejoice every day I work with these two Taras.

Energetic effort is a surprise weapon in our contra-worrying arsenal. When I'm completely focused on what I am doing, it is impossible to worry. Joy can then seep up through the cracks in my consciousness. I have no idea why this is true.

Quiet time also allows for the upward seeping of joy. Quiet time seems like such a small thing. But, oh, the windows it opens! Watching the dance of diamonds on a cold winter's night. Spending a morning in the back corner of a yard, weeding. Just saying no to the iPod for some natural-noises time. Washing dishes mindfully. Meditating every morning before the sun rises and then heading out to walk the dog while it is still quiet. Every day joy gets its shot at taking over our brains when we give it some quiet space to show up. As it does, for me, I can't believe how lucky I am, even in the months when the bills multiply on my countertop behind my back.

There is plenty of joy for each of us. It's just looking for openings. The least we can do is provide them.

ten

The Whole World Is Our Garden: Vigilance

Now we know, we are all brothers
Now we know, we are all sisters
Now we know, we share the earth
Now we know, our touch is green.
—Litha Sovell of Tanzania

Seattle is a city of gardens. People brag about the ones they know, and rightly so. Just when you think you've seen the most beautiful garden possible, someone will casually mention one you haven't heard about—the Bellevue Botanical Garden or maybe the E. B. Dunn Historical Garden or the handful of private gardens on islands like Whidbey that cause people like Martha Stewart to fly in just to see them.

What you don't expect to see is a garden tucked away behind one of the city's toughest neighborhoods. But it is there. Driving from the center of the city south is like traveling through history. Signs on storefronts morph from Vietnamese to Spanish and back. *Tiendas* sit next to noodle shops. They both sit next to auto shops. Grates cover windows. Many of the cars on the side streets look abandoned. They aren't. Buildings are two or three stories and badly need painting. People hurry when they walk.

Driving up a hill into the south end of the neighborhood, I was lost. Pulling over to check a map, I saw a sign for Kubota Garden. I decided to be nosy and found a parking lot big enough for maybe a hundred cars. A huge bulletin board was at the entrance. On the bulletin board was a haiku, welcoming visitors:

A caterpillar
this deep in fall—
still not a butterfly

Behind the bulletin board, huge formal gates, as big as temple gates, opened onto a landscape straight out of Wonderland. At first it looked like a sea of every green imaginable, complemented by reds, yellows, and golds. And there were twenty acres of this beauty. A quiet walk along the park's trails took me past streams, waterfalls, ponds, and carefully placed mammoth garden rocks. Two bright red, rounded bridges crossed the streams.

The park is a testament to vigilance.

In 1907 Fujitaro Kubota moved from Japan to the Northwest to start a gardening company. He was so talented that his company, the

Kubota Gardening Company, was very successful. Examples of his work can still be seen throughout metropolitan Seattle, from the gardens that make up Seattle University's campus to the Bloedel Reserve on Bainbridge Island.

After twenty years of working in the United States, Fujitaro decided to create a garden he could share with other city residents. He started out with five acres of what was basically logged-off swampland. Over time the five acres grew and his garden became a social gathering place for Seattle's Japanese community.

All this stopped in World War II. Kubota, his wife, and his sons were taken to Camp Minidoka in Idaho, where they stayed for the entire war. The garden was abandoned. When Kubota returned to Seattle, he picked up where he had left off, rebuilding both his business and the garden. With his sons he brought in over four hundred tons of stone to create a mountainside, complete with waterfalls and reflection pools. He never quit building the garden. It shows.

Fujitaro died in 1973. He was ninety-four. When his property was later targeted for condominium developments, the neighborhood fought back in his name. Finally, in 1981 his property was declared a historic landmark and opened to the public.

As you walk along its trails, Fujitaro's spirit is palpable. The sheer beauty of each view is the result of his deeply thoughtful choices about which plants should go where, and how to position pools so that water best reflects the beauty of the property. His streams bring sounds and birdsong into the garden, and the quiet pools reflect Seattle's ever-changing sky, providing the sensation of movement where there is none. Kubota's smells are the smells of the Northwest, clean and clear, pine filled and just this side of sweet. There is a strong feeling of serenity and peace, smack in the middle of a neighborhood struggling to survive.

One of the things a Kubota garden visitor walks away with is a deeper appreciation of trees. Yulan magnolias. Maples with names like "Pacific Sunset." Giant dogwoods sixty feet tall. Rare maples from the north of China—the ones that turn both pale orange and red in the fall. Cedars. Asian holly. English yew. Colorado spruce. Maybe a visit will mark the beginning of a lifelong love affair, or maybe an existing love affair will grow. Maybe you will become a rabid environmentalist.

That would be auspicious given that we're losing our trees.

A photograph I have hanging over my desk shows four women holding hands as they are wrapped around a huge tree. The women are wearing long skirts and saris. Three of them have covered their heads. They are Indian, I think, and young. They are tree huggers determined to save us from our penchant for deforestation. In India alone, the loss of trees has led to floods and the crippling of local economies. People have died as a result. Villages have been lost. So now, no more. These women are willing to give their lives if they have to. In other parts of the world, the same. Monks in Thailand have wrapped saffron cloth around trees to mark them as sacred. In this way some might be saved from the megalogging that is now moving through Southeast Asia.

The Buddhist sutras tell a story about the Buddha actually yelling at some travelers who, after they took shelter under a tree, cut it down. He is really mad. Our job is to promote life, not destroy it.

Time to step in.

I ask myself, "How can I help?" I can buy trees and plants for friends as gifts. Done. I can donate money to someone who will plant trees where they are needed. Done again. It doesn't take much. I can grow a garden, to replenish both myself and the Earth. Vegetable gardens are easy to grow and, given my lawn-caring clumsiness, much easier to take care of than a front or backyard. And the smells? Oh, yes, the smells. Basil. Rosemary. Thyme. Warm-season vegetables like tomatoes, cucumbers, green peppers, and onions are almost too easy to grow. Cool-season vegetables will take me right into winter: cabbages, kale, radishes. All I have to do is make sure the soil drains so the poor things don't drown while they are busy starting to grow, then keep them moist until they sprout. After that it is regular watering and weed patrol, and I'm in fresh vegetables for most of the year.

Or we can find other people and support their efforts. Women like Wangari Maathai, for example. She is one of the reasons I haven't given up on the fate of the planet. This woman makes my heart sing.

Born the third of six children, Maathai started life in 1940 in the central highlands of what was then British Kenya. Her family's mud-walled house didn't have electricity or running water. Her family kept cattle, goats, and sheep. Seasons were predictable—rainy and not-rainy. The rainy season made the earth lush, and from the way Maathai talks about them, the people were happy. Her father was so strong, "he didn't need a jack to change the wheel of his car." Her mother, tall and thin, was sturdy, hardworking, gentle, and quiet. Her father worked for a British landowner until Kenya's independence. With his four wives and ten children, he was a true patriarch. The family owned twenty-five acres that they used for vegetables and grazing for their animals.

When Maathai was seven she was sent to Nyeri with her mother and youngest sister, where she watched the colonial government burn off national forests, trading them for non-native trees, which grew fast, were commercially successful, and sucked the energy right out of the land. The area's ecosystem was crippled so badly that rivers and streams dried up and underground water almost disappeared.

During the same period, a war of resistance to British rule surfaced, forcing the little girl to lead a life of hiding from raids. Nearly a million Kenyans were interred in concentration camps. By 1954 three out of every four native men were in some form of jail. The land was taken from their families. Maathai and her mother were forced to live in an "emergency village," where they stayed for the next seven years. Unlike many of the "villagers," they survived.

Maathai was able to continue her schooling, graduating from high school at the top of her class. From there she attended university in the United States, thanks to Senator John F. Kennedy's Airlift Africa program. A graduate degree in biology from the University of Pittsburgh opened the door to a university job back in Kenya. There she met her future husband, Mwangi Maathai. After time out to earn a doctorate in Germany, Wangari married in 1969, at twenty-nine. Her husband began a successful political career, and they settled down to have a family. By 1977 Maathai was hitting her professional stride as an associate professor of veterinary medicine.

During this time she became more and more concerned about the environment. Rivers continued to dry up. Trees were still being cut down to make room for growing coffee and tea. The loss of the trees made firewood impossible to find. As a result, families started turning to more and more processed foods—white bread, rice, and flour—for their meals. This, in turn, led to soaring rates of malnutrition, especially among children and the elderly: "The connection between the symptoms of environmental degradation and their causes—deforestation, devegetation, unsustainable agriculture, and soil loss were self evident. Something had to be done.... It just came to me: 'Why not plant trees?'" (Wangari Maathai, *Unbowed: A Memoir* [New York: Knopf, 2006], 125).

Trees would provide the firewood families needed to cook nutritious meals. Trees meant shade and roots that could protect watersheds. Trees could provide food. They could bring back the birds.

The Green Belt Movement began. Maathai started planting trees, hiring teams of people who would descend on a garden and, in a day, transform it with new, strong trees. After a few false starts, farmers, schools, and churches became involved in her effort. Mobil Oil gave her money. The Canadian ambassador to Kenya gave her a car. She decided that she wanted to plant a tree for every person in Kenya.

The true heroes of her movement were the women of Kenya. They just kept planting trees. When they ran out of seedlings, they grew more from seeds. Some groups committed to planting at least a thousand trees as greenbelts capable of restoring the Earth to "its cloth of green."

To say that life became difficult for Maathai as all this unfolded would be the understatement of this book. Her husband left her, and because she defended herself during the divorce proceedings, she was thrown into jail with only a pail to use as a toilet and a blanket for company.

At forty-one, Maathai was left with a tiny bungalow she had purchased as a vacation house and three children to raise. What did she do? Plant trees.

She organized a march in support of renewable resources and was given support from two surprise sources, the Norwegian Forestry Society and the United Nations Voluntary Fund for Women. The people whose lives she was touching started to see the connections between the new crops they were growing, notably coffee and tea, and the soil erosion that was happening. They began to see the connection between trees disappearing and the loss of basic human rights.

By the middle of the decade, nearly two thousand women's groups were planting and lending trees, and more than a thousand greenbelts were being cared for by students and schools. Together they had planted several million trees. Eventually more than six thousand nurseries were established and more than thirty million trees were planted in Kenya alone.

A revolution was taking shape. When the government decided to close off one of the country's largest parks, Uhuru Park in Nairobi, so it could be developed, protests reopened the park. Because she was one of the protest leaders, Maathai was targeted by the government and thrown back into jail. This time she almost died. When word got out that she was in jail and very sick, support came from around the world, including the United States. Eight U.S. senators, including Al Gore and Edward M. Kennedy, wrote to President Moi of Kenya that arresting prodemocracy figures could damage relations between the two countries. Maathai was sent home.

The 1990s in Kenya were extremely dangerous. Mothers watched as their politically active sons were thrown into jail without recourse. Fifty women decided to go on a public hunger strike in protest. Even with threats and rumors of torture, they stayed. By the fourth day, policemen appeared with tear gas and batons. The women didn't move. Finally, the police came and carried each one away. Maathai was beaten so badly she was hospitalized. Some of the women who had been able to get away from the police were given sanctuary in All Saints Cathedral, an Anglican church. There they continued their hunger strike for a year.

The cathedral became Maathai's second home. She focused her energy into writing the stories of the women's sons while soldiers surrounded the church. When the women were afraid that the soldiers were planning to come in, they chained themselves together. In 1993 all but one of the young men were released. The last one was released in 1997.

Meanwhile, to save her own life, Maathai went into hiding. Through friends she sent messages out to the world at every opportunity, telling us that ethnic cleansing was going on in Kenya. Amnesty International took up her cause, sending out an urgent action alert to all of its members. Those who could left Kenya. Many settled in Norway because of its support of the green movement. Then, in 2004, the Nobel Peace Prize winner was announced: Wangari Maathai. By then she had won a seat in Parliament based on a political platform she called the three legs of a stool:

The need for respecting human rights
The need for sustainable and equitable management of resources
The need for a culture of peace

Since then, progress. Since then, greenbelts.

⤳

You never know where Earth-loving tree protectors will surface. Michael Lehnert is a major general in the U.S. Marine Corps. At first blush, he seems an unlikely environmentalist. If you look more closely, his sense of environmental stewardship is palpable. As I write, he is stationed at Camp Pendleton, which takes up almost two hundred square miles between San Diego and Los Angeles, California. Located within the boundaries of the camp are a coastal plain, a coastal valley, and a mountain. Much of the land is undeveloped. As a result, the place teems with wildlife. At least eighteen endangered species live on the land—from the California least tern to the arroyo toad.

Lehnert is the camp's commander, responsible for getting the forty thousand men and women under his command ready for combat. He does that. He also has eighty-four staff working to protect the area: "It's possible to find ways to get marines ready for combat and at the same time be good stewards. It's not a zero-sum game to me.... A country worth defending is a country worth preserving" (From "A Few Good Species" by Marilyn Berlin Snell, *Sierra Magazine*, November/December 2006, 23).

The marines fight soil erosion. They purify water with solar panels and restore vernal pools. The general does these things in spite of the Department of Defense's reputation for requesting exemptions from major environmental laws. He goes after invasive plants like the giant reed, arundo. Marines have cleared the arundo from the base's property line to the ocean. Nine miles of clearing.

He has worked with the Sierra Club on projects and plans to continue protecting terrain critical to "birds and beasties." The general is vigilance personified, protecting the Earth he clearly loves in wonderful, creative ways.

Seeds and seedlings grow into forests step by step. In this growing they have the capacity to support societies where every single person is honored. All you and I need to do is start planting the seeds. This is a small doing. One simple act followed by the next simple act, resting when we need to rest, admiring what we need to admire. Seeds to gardens, gardens to forests, forests to seeds to gardens, in an exquisite dance.

So it is with a happy life for each one of us. Happiness is there for the taking. A good life, one that nurtures us, is like a seed yearning to be watered. Like a seed, it doesn't take much to kick things into gear.

None of this means our lives will be easy. This work is hard work. Happily, Shantideva gives us the tools we need to make perfect gardens of our lives anyway. He tells us to have intention and to enthusiastically move in the direction of that intention, trusting ourselves. He instructs us to be generous, to stop feeding our anger, and to be as patient as a tree reaching its way to the sky. He demands that we let joy in and that we stay vigilant in our efforts. If we follow these teachings, small doing by small doing, joy is ours. I promise you, miracles will happen.

In our gardens there will be constant weeds. Okay. In our heads there will be weeds, as well. Okay again. We pull them once, twice, ten thousand times—because we can. Because we must. Get out there and get dirty, my friend. Nothing matters more.

May you be fearless. May you make your life breathtakingly beautiful through your acts of generosity and compassion. May these same acts make the world a cleaner and safer place for the children of our children. Small acts writ large change history. Wangari Maathai's life is proof of this. So is yours. For me, simply sitting in meditation has cleared out so many mind-weeds that, almost neurosis free, I have time and energy to simply be of service, one seedling at a time. In the book *The Impossible Will Take a Little While,* there is a story about a woman who, in the early 1960s, took two of her kids to a vigil in front of the White House. They were protesting nuclear testing. It was pouring rain. Only about a hundred people, mostly women and children, took part in the vigil. Years later she attended a major march where baby doctor Benjamin Spock spoke out against testing. When someone asked him how he got involved in this issue given all the demands on his time, he responded that years earlier he had seen a small group of women standing in the rain, huddled with their children in front of the White House, protesting nuclear testing. "I thought if those women were out there, their cause must be really important" (*The Impossible Will Take a Little While,* ed. Paul Rogat Loeb [New York: Basic Books, 2004], 7).

Lord, who can be trusted with power

and who may act in your place?

Those with a passion for justice,

Who speak the truth from their hearts;

Who have let go of selfish interests

And grown beyond their own lives;

Who see the wretched as their family

And the poor as their flesh and blood.

They alone are impartial

And worthy of the people's trust.

Their compassion lights up the whole earth,

And their kindness endures forever.

—Psalm 15, Stephen Mitchell, *A Book of Psalms*
  (New York: HarperCollins, 1993), 7

May you be happy beyond your wildest dreams.

May 21, 2007

Ten nature- and garden-related books that convey the sweet feeling that a life filled with small doings can bring

In the middle of writing *Plant Seed, Pull Weed*, it dawned on me that, at fifty-seven, my days as a landscaper could come to a screeching halt at any time. To prove to myself that it is possible to get the same sense of sweet contentedness that comes from working mindfully in the dirt without actually digging, I went on what only can be described as an obsessed hunt for books that convey that deep sense of well-being. Hundreds of books later, here are ten. If each one were a person, I would ask it to go steady.

- *Seeds from a Birch Tree: Writing Haiku and the Spiritual Journey* by Clark Strand (New York: Hyperion, 1997) is ostensibly about haiku. It is also about gardens and dirt and seeing clearly. If most books with gardening themes are milk chocolate, Strand's is 80 percent cocoa. Best savored slowly with tea.

- *Pilgrim at Tinker Creek* by Annie Dillard (1974; reprint, New York: HarperPerennial, 1998) is about a year living in a valley in Virginia's Blue Ridge Mountains. Dillard wrote the book in her twenties and received the Pulitzer Prize for it at the ripe old age of twenty-nine. Her aliveness is both palpable and comforting. Good to read with a hearty soup and thick chunk of dark bread.

- *A Sand County Almanac* by Aldo Leopold, photos by Michael Sewell, (1949; reprint, New York: Oxford University Press, 1987) is still a touching read, even though it was written over fifty years ago. As a young man, Leopold worked for the forest service, later becoming a respected professor at the University of Wisconsin. His almanac, published a year after he died, is a valentine to nature. It reads like a journal, starting in January, when Leopold responds to the beginning thaws of spring, moving through the season of trout, and back into winter. The November essay, "If I Were the Wind," is a love song. Reading it, I wanted to make a cup of pine needle tea like that served in the mountains of South Korea.

- *My Garden (Book)* by Jamaica Kincaid (New York: Farrar Straus Giroux, 1999) is just plain fun. Shortly before Kincaid became a mother for the first time, her husband gave her a hoe, a rake, a spade, a fork, and some flower seeds. *My Garden (Book)* is the story of her discovery of all things gardening. Kincaid is such a masterful storyteller that it is difficult to read the book at a leisurely pace. Her description of the Chelsea Flower Show and its characters is worth the price of the book all by itself. Best just to grab an espresso, and maybe a walnut biscotti, and hunker down prepared to not look up again until the last page.

- *One Man's Garden* by Henry Mitchell (Boston: Houghton Mifflin, 1992). Mitchell wrote the "Earthman" column for the *Washington*

Post for over twenty years way back when. He loves and knows gardens. What is great about Mitchell is that he is hilariously grumpy: "People who say disgusting things are often right." This book is a collection of essays organized into the twelve months of the year. He covers everything from the fallacy of maintenance-free gardens to insisting that a reasonable tomato harvest needs only two plants per adult. Mitchell gives direct advice throughout. Best read in winter in a week when you are sure spring will never come.

- *Garden Open Today* by Beverley Nichols (1963; Portland: Timber Press, 2002). Okay, some of the plant names have changed in the nearly fifty years since the book was first published, and some of his chemical applications are now illegal. Nichols is a delight anyway. He is the sun to Mitchell's moon, invariably upbeat. The best part of this book is that he invites readers to visit his home garden, where he kept his promise to keep it open until he died in 1983. Nichols can also be a smart aleck in the best sense of the word. "Gardening gloves may be all very well in their way, but in so many tasks, like weeding, one has literally to take the gloves off. Only one's own nails and fingers can deal, for example, with the sinister little bulbous roots of *Oxalis floribunda*." Amen, brother.

- *Green Thoughts: A Writer in the Garden* by Eleanor Perényi (1981; reprint, New York: Modern Library, 2002) is a classic. It is a book made up of smart and spunky essays, seventy-two to be exact, covering everything from earthworms to rock gardens with some sexual politics thrown in for spice. Perényi has the capacity to infuse the reader with happiness through her words. Plus, she is quite the romantic figure in her own right, having been married to a Hungarian baron ("I have had only two gardens in my life. The first was a large rather mournful park ... attached to my husband's castle in Hungary") before moving to the not-so-windswept coast of Connecticut.

- *The Wild Braid: A Poet Reflects on a Century in the Garden* by Stanley Kunitz with Genine Lentine, photos by Marnie Crawford (New York: Norton, 2005), is a book of photographs as much as it is a book of words. In 2005 Stanley Kunitz turned one hundred years old. For most of his century he wrote poetry that won just about every award poetry can get, from the Pulitzer Prize to the National Medal of the Arts. It turns out that Kunitz was also an extraordinary gardener and, until he died in 2006, could be found almost daily in his seaside garden in Provincetown, Massachusetts: "All my life, the garden has been a great teacher in everything I cherish." This is a book to read over and over, so you might as well buy it.

- *From the Ground Up: The Story of a First Garden* by Amy Stewart (Chapel Hill, NC: Algonquin Books, 2001). The author of *Flower Confidential* tells the story of how a twelve-hundred-square-foot patch of land was transformed inch by inch. Stewart writes with a sweet openheartedness, admitting from the start that she is a "daughter of the suburbs where flowers come in cellophane and spinach in frozen blocks." Her book is a quiet story of transformation as she learns as much about herself as she does about gardening while she works. This seems to be the nature of gardening. Part of Stewart's charm is that, in addition to her wry sense of humor, she is fearless about inserting her strong opinions about plants into her narrative: "Nandina, a dull, unimaginative shrub with leaves the color of cockroaches." I dare you not to cry when you read her letter to the next gardener, the one she leaves behind when she moves north.

- *Paths of Desire: The Passions of a Suburban Gardener* by Dominique Browning (New York: Scribner, 2004) is a different take on gardening. It is more about the power of gardens to buffer us as we wade through the heartbreaks of our lives, whether the loss of a lover or a marriage or saying good-bye to a child now grown and leaving home. Browning, who when she wrote this book had been the editor-in-chief of *House and Garden* since 1995, feels like an old friend from her first paragraph. Covering a time span of fifteen years, she describes the Westchester, New York, garden that starts out as that of a young mother, becomes a garden of a woman at the end of her marriage, and finally that of a woman once again filled with wonder and whisperings of happiness. Part of her allure is that Browning is wonderfully self-effacing. She forgets the names of plants—even the most familiar ones—the way the rest of us can.

She wrestles with concrete retaining walls that collapse in the night; with sassafras trees that have taken over her front yard; with neighbors who leave trash as large as an old VW bus up against her back fence. She puts up with a lover who is mostly absent and—forgive me, Dominique—is a jerk. You should have dumped him at his first disappearance. I'm certain Buddha agrees with me. Through all her upsets, I loved this book and was sad when it ended.